TEN LESSONS
IN LEADERSHIP AND LEARNING

An Educator's Journey

John D'Auria

ISBN: 978-1-62249-515-3

Published by
The Educational Publisher
Biblio Publishing
Columbus, Ohio
BiblioPublishing.com

Copyright © 2010 by *TEACHERS*[21]
All rights reserved. No part of this book may be reproduced in any manner whatsoever without the prior written permission of the author.

To order copies of this book or to request reprint permission, please contact:

TEACHERS[21]
34 Washington Street, Wellesley, MA 02481
781-416-0980
Teachers21.org

TABLE OF CONTENTS

Introduction 1

Overview of the Ten Lessons 3

Lesson One 7
    Foster a climate that nurtures constant growth and improvement

Lesson Two 13
    Develop and promote new mindsets about learning

Lesson Three 29
    Cultivate core values

Lesson Four 37
    Understand that professional relationships are the engine of change

Lesson Five 41
    Courageously address nondiscussables

Lesson Six 47
    Exercise emotional intelligence

Lesson Seven 57
    Transform difficult conversations into understanding and better informed decisions

Lesson Eight 69
    Use meetings (of all types) to increase academic focus

Lesson Nine 75
    Remember the choices that constantly present themselves

Lesson Ten 81
    Recognize that leadership is an improvisational art

Conclusion 91

Appendix 95

Bibliography 107

ACKNOWLEDGEMENTS

Over my years in schools, I have had the privilege of working with outstanding educators from whom I have learned immensely. The following educators were especially important in shaping my insights and observations:

> My colleagues and collaborators, **Jon Saphier** and **Matt King**, provided many thoughtful insights through the conversations that yielded the DNA of Leadership and our joint articles.

> In her role as Director of Curriculum and Instruction for the Wellesley, Massachusetts Public Schools, **Judy Boroschek** taught me the importance of skillful instruction and a robust curriculum.

> My wife, **Ann D'Auria,** a highly skillful teacher, taught me many lessons about the importance of emotions and the vital information embedded in them.

My parents, **Fernanda D'Auria** and **Pelliegrino (Daniel) D'Auria,** also contributed to my development as an educator through the high value they placed on education and the sacrifices they made to support my learning.

Many people have also contributed significantly to the conceptualization and development of this book. **Susan Freedman** has continuously encouraged me with her insights on the importance of writing down these ideas. She has been a guiding hand throughout this process. Her support has been invaluable. **Barbara Aschheim's** skillful editing helped me to clarify my message and bring precision to my language. Helping a writer say more with fewer words is a gift that Barbara possesses. **Richard Deppe** was one of the early readers of the text. His keen eye and experience as an educational leader provided me with the confidence to successfully meet the challengwes that writing can pose. My children, **Elizabeth O'Connor** and **Michael D'Auria,** have helped me to appreciate the intimate connection between parenting and teaching. The support they have provided has fueled my desire to pass on the nuggets in these lessons to future generations of teachers, leaders, and parents.

INTRODUCTION

In 1971 I started teaching math in East Boston, Massachusetts. Personal computers did not exist. The Internet was not available. Special education was not a program in our schools. Girls were not encouraged to play sports or enter many careers that were considered solely the domain of men. In 2007, I became the superintendent of a school district south of Boston. During these thirty-six years, technology has transformed many, if not most, aspects of our lives. Our knowledge base about learning disabilities has grown exponentially. The walls separating the genders have become thinner. Our President is an African American— a fact that would have been inconceivable when I entered the teaching profession. Within this four-decade period, I have been a teacher, guidance counselor, principal, superintendent, and parent. Each of these roles has provided insights and a unique perspective on both learning and leadership during this amazing period of change.

This book offers ten significant lessons for educational leaders that I have distilled from my experience, from the research literature, and from my professional collaborations. While the main focus of the lessons is aimed at educators, there are ideas and insights that will be helpful to parents, coaches, and others who are involved in the growth and development of young people.

At first glance, the lessons are out of sync with many state and federal initiatives. You will not read about test scores, performance pay, or new technologies for transforming schools into 21st Century institutions. I believe that focusing on the lessons illuminated in this text will create learning environments in which teachers continually and thoughtfully improve their craft. As an extension, I believe that the outcome for students will be that they focus on their areas of weakness without embarrassment or shame as they challenge themselves to excel.

Ultimately, many of the current initiatives for improving education in the United States are aimed at having our schools develop smarter, better-educated students. In order to achieve this goal, however, we must develop a common understanding of what we mean by smart and better educated. If we conceive of smart as achieving a certain level on a standard test, we will be selling the next generation short. Test scores, while helpful in calibrating growth and providing indications of how to improve skills, may mask weaknesses or misrepresent strengths. Most importantly, test scores are silent about the creativity, collaboration, perseverance, resilience, and flexibility in thinking that will be required of students in the workplace and as citizens and parents. This limitation, however, should not cause us to throw out quantitative data. We have other approaches, explored in these lessons, that enable us to avoid using test score analysis as our primary lens for describing growth, development, progress, and all of the other elements of a good education.

It is difficult to criticize our current national conversation about education without sounding like an old educator who wants to return to a time and a place that no longer exists. My contentions and beliefs are firmly rooted in the present with a look toward the future. My insights are based on what I see in the eyes and countenances of current classroom teachers, principals, and 21st Century students who are in the front line of modern day schooling.

The Ten Lessons suggest that leaders must:

1. Foster a climate that nurtures constant growth and improvement
2. Develop and promote new mindsets about learning
3. Cultivate core values
4. Understand that professional relationships are the engine of change
5. Courageously address nondiscussables
6. Exercise emotional intelligence
7. Transform difficult conversations into understanding
8. Use meetings (of all types) to increase academic focus
9. Remember the choices that constantly present themselves
10. Recognize that leadership is an improvisational art

Overview of the Ten Lessons

Each of the following ten lessons contains an important insight that is central to effective leadership. These lessons are presented briefly in this overview.

LESSON ONE

Foster a climate that nurtures constant growth and improvement

Once a leader establishes a climate or culture that promotes learning, growth, and improvement, a school system becomes flexible enough to adapt to the future and changing needs of students. The system becomes malleable. As students with unfamiliar learning disabilities enter the schools, as technology shifts to impact teaching differently, as curricular or pedagogical emphases change, staff who have internalized and embraced a culture of continual growth are positioned to meet these changing needs.

Similarly, a school's culture impacts students. Cultures that emphasize improvement and growth over test scores encourage students to work on their weaknesses, overcome setbacks and obstacles, and develop the habits of mind that produce resiliency and a desire for mastery. Lesson One is pivotal in this framework of ten leadership responsibilities because it provides the environment on which all of the others depend.

In using the terms culture and climate interchangeably, I am referencing a set of learned beliefs, values, and behaviors that relate to how people interact within a particular society, organization, or group. In these lessons, culture and climate imply shared norms, rules, and ways that people work together.

LESSON TWO

Develop and promote new mindsets about learning

One of the ways to achieve a climate that is focused on learning, improvement, and development is by promoting a "growth mindset" that highlights the effort and strategies required for achievement. This approach negates native ability as the prime factor that determines the ability to achieve. With a growth mindset, people are able to learn new approaches, new strategies, and new techniques without the shame and embarrassment that can sometimes obstruct growth. A growth mindset encourages learning because it diminishes the influence of the inevitable mistakes and setbacks that learners encounter.

LESSON THREE
Cultivate core values

Core values answer the question, "What does this school stand for?" Responding to this question in a manner that is both genuine and authentic provides energy for getting through difficult times. It establishes a unique voice that lets the school community communicate effectively with its constituencies. Core values are an important means of both enhancing the culture of the school community and guiding its direction. Core values help a school community remain true to its vision as it encounters the innumerable challenges and dilemmas that are part of school life.

LESSON FOUR
Understand that professional relationships are the engine of change

Professional relationships generate human energy that can move a system forward or obstruct its progress toward its academic and social goals. These relationships are especially critical when they facilitate open and honest communication among people with differences of opinion and divergent ways of thinking.

LESSON FIVE
Courageously address nondiscussables

It is difficult to develop an atmosphere in which controversial and "hard to talk about" topics are discussed openly and honestly. Developing this atmosphere is a key component in making effective change in schools.

LESSON SIX

Exercise emotional intelligence

While the main focus of the work of schools is the mind, the heart plays a vital role in learning. There are inevitable frustrations that occur when mastery and success are not easily achieved. Educators who understand emotional "data" and interpret it insightfully will be more successful as leaders.

LESSON SEVEN

Transform difficult conversations into understanding and better informed decisions

There are three skill sets that are essential for managing the complexities of relationships and maneuvering successfully through the conflicts that are an inherent aspect of school communities. These skill sets are described and explored in this lesson.

LESSON EIGHT

Use meetings (of all types) to increase academic focus

Professional development is increasingly designed as learning opportunities that are ongoing and embedded in the workplace. Meetings, if constructed thoughtfully and managed successfully, can provide an effective forum for professional development. The "regular" work of meetings should be focused on helping educators who are struggling to solve problems, improve lesson plans, strengthen learning experiences, and achieve more success with students.

LESSON NINE

Remember the choices that constantly present themselves

Leaders inevitably face choices that are less than visible to colleagues and stakeholders. Understanding with clarity what these options are can help a leader understand the importance of high expectations, vision, courage, and efficacy. These personal qualities are essential for effective leadership but are not the qualities explicitly taught to aspiring administrators.

LESSON TEN

Recognize that leadership is an improvisational art

Leadership is a domain that demands creative thinking, long and short time planning, and the ability to think on one's feet. There is no easy formula for effective leadership.

These Ten Lessons are interrelated and require applications that are nuanced to the leader's particular context. Each lesson provides a strategic means for strengthening the academic focus of a school community. The domains described in the lessons are ones that are sometimes overlooked or under represented in the reform literature. These lessons must be examined and worked on by school leaders and staff. If continuous attention is not paid to these domains, efforts aimed at improving a school's performance will be like pouring water into a colander. There will be little effort or success that is sustained.

Lesson ONE

"Keep in mind your overarching goal: to create an atmosphere where constant growth and improvement occurs. An essential pre-requisite for this to happen is that people honestly discuss where they are struggling, where they are uncertain, where they have concerns. This is the basic form of a learning community."
John D'Auria, Opening Address to Administrators, Canton, MA, August, 2009

While contexts vary significantly from town to town and state-to-state in America, optimizing the teaching resources that exist in communities is a constant that will give students the best chance to obtain a quality education. While some communities suffer from insufficient resources, even more are affected by the inefficient utilization of the resources that exist. Leaders have the dual role of advocating for the resources needed and optimizing the resources they already have.

Foster a climate that nurtures constant growth and improvement

LEADERSHIP RESOURCES

Optimization is central to Lesson One. In order to maximize resource utilization, a leader must develop a climate or culture that nurtures, encourages, demands, and sustains continual improvement. While technology and 21st Century tools can help support this culture, technology is not a central factor in climate control. The climate is communicated through the behaviors, reactions, thinking, and messages of the leader. It is a highly human domain. There are no short cuts. Climate cannot be created and nurtured long distance or off site. Climate control is the primary responsibility of leaders and supersedes all other objectives.

Haim Ginott, a teacher, child psychologist, and author of the book, *Teacher and Child: A Book for Parents and Teachers*, writes:

I've come to a frightening conclusion that I am the decisive element in the classroom. It is my personal approach that creates the climate. It's my daily mood that makes the weather. As a teacher I have tremendous power to make a child's life miserable or joyous. I can be a tool of torture or an instrument of inspiration.

> *I can humiliate or humor, hurt or heal. In all situations, it is my response that decides whether a crisis will be escalated or deescalated and a child humanized or dehumanized.*

This quote eloquently captures the power and potential that teachers have to create a climate within their area of responsibility - a climate that affects children no differently than a sunny day can brighten our outlook or a rainy day can dampen our mood. Parents of school age children understand this notion intuitively. They attend an open house, have a conversation with a teacher, and listen carefully to the comments of their kids. These experiences give them an impression of the kind of atmosphere that their children are exposed to within a classroom. How a teacher responds to mistakes, the tone of voice expressed in engaging students, and the approach used in communicating expectations are indicators that describe the climate established within a particular teacher's domain.

While a great deal has been written about the strategies that teachers can employ to craft a responsive and thriving climate or classroom culture, we know less about the ways this climate can be established by educational leaders within their spheres of influence. Yet, developing a vibrant and thriving work climate is an important responsibility of leadership. Schools are systems. The learning environment in a particular classroom is often influenced by the more encompassing climate or culture that has been established within a department, a school, and an entire district.

My colleague, Matt King, and I have altered the original Ginott quote to describe this aspect of leadership:

> *We've come to the conclusion that a leader is the decisive element in the school community. It is the personal approach of that leader which creates the climate. It's the emotional responses of the leader that make the weather. The leader has tremendous power to make the life of teachers and students miserable or joyous. The leader can be a tool of torture or an instrument of inspiration. He or she can humiliate or humor, hurt or heal. In all situations, it is the reactions of the leader that decide whether a crisis will be escalated or deescalated and a community strengthened or diminished."*

LESSON ONE

One of the most important lessons that I have learned as an educator is that a leader's effectiveness is grounded in his or her ability to create an atmosphere that brings out the best in people and leads its members to continually improve. Roland Barth writes, "Unless teachers and administrators act to change the culture of a school, all innovations, high standards, and high-stakes tests will have to fit in and around existing elements of the culture. They will remain superficial window dressing incapable of making much of a difference." Barth continues, "For, as we know, more than anything else, it is the culture of the school that determines the achievement of teacher and student alike."

POSITIVE SCHOOL CLIMATE AND STUDENT ACHIEVEMENT

While many would support the potential benefits for adults that result from a positive work climate, recent studies are now pointing to the link between such climates and student achievement. Establishing a positive school climate is not just a means of helping teachers feel enthusiastic about their work; it is a vital tool for supporting improved achievement of students. In "Successful School Restructuring," Newmann and Wehlage note that if the performance of two "average" students were compared - one in a school with low teacher professional community and the other in a school with high professional community - the students in the high community school would score about 27% higher on the performance measures used. The authors cite another study that focused on the level of professional community and its effects on student achievement in 800 high schools. The researchers found that in schools in which teachers reported higher levels of collective responsibility for student learning, achievement was greater in math, science, reading, and history. Bryk and Schneider, in a study entitled "Trust in Schools: A Core Resource for Improvement," found that schools reporting strong trust links (a complex dynamic in which parties depend on one another and on a shared vision) were three times more likely to report eventual improvements in reading and math scores than those in which trust levels were low. Elbot and Fulton, quoting Michael Fullan in "Building an Intentional School Culture: Excellence in Academics and Character," note that out of "134 secondary schools in England that were part of the 2004 Hay Group study, the successful schools had a much more demanding culture - while the less successful schools had less of a press on improvement and were more forgiving if results were not forthcoming."

Department heads, principals, and superintendents are often curious about how to influence the tone and culture within their domain. Central to this work is the question: "What are the levers a leader can move in order to affect the climate?" For too long, the prevailing notion has been that climate is a direct function of a leader's personality or the immutable context that historically shaped the school. As part of this framework, many believe that a vibrant culture cannot be created without installing a charismatic leader or removing entrenched veteran teachers. Recent research studies (Deal & Peterson, 2009; Lucas & Valentine, 2002), in combination with years of school experience, confirm that shaping a climate is a skill that can be taught, learned, and can impact a wide range of contexts.

Culture building requires access to a complex skill set that demands nuanced interventions and improvisational interpretations by a leader. It is a challenging task for educators to change their practice in order to improve their impact on students. However, this skill set is eminently teachable and many of its strategies and skills are applicable to environments within and outside of schools.

Four important factors have emerged as significant in shaping a culture:

1. A growth mindset about learning
2. A set of genuine and vital core values
3. High quality professional relationships within an institution
4. Productive meetings that engage adult learners in thinking about complex issues and questions

It is easy to name these four important ingredients of culture building. It is harder to understand them at a deep level and apply this knowledge to the context of a particular school or district. Each of these cultural components is like an iceberg; it has a visible part that is easy to spot but there is much subtlety that lies beneath the surface. Each factor is made up of a vast network of interconnected skills that a leader must acquire. Strengthening the quality of professional relationships, for example, involves applying skills and insights such as emotional intelligence, conflict resolution, open and honest communication, and the management of difficult conversations.

Culture is also shaped by how leaders go about solving the problems they encounter in their environments. Big or small, complex or simple, short or long term, every problem presents leaders with "teachable moments" that unwrap:

- Their beliefs about learning
- Their beliefs about what it means to be smart
- The degree to which they value (or don't value) collaboration, trust, and respect
- Their commitment to understanding the root causes of a problem
- The benefits of a healthy curiosity
- The importance of listening well
- The value of paying attention to what is said and to what goes unstated

Culture is created, moment by moment, by how leaders interact with others and their environments. The verbal and non verbal communications that occur within these interactions, along with the thinking, collaboration, experimentation, and creativity that potentially emerge from these "moments," add an atom which combines with other atoms from previous encounters to form a molecule. Over time, a cultural pattern is formed that reflects the quality of these interactions. This teaching-grappling-learning approach is replicated by teachers as they work with their students who, in turn, embrace the connection between learning and continual improvement. This is the power and the potential of a learning culture.

The degree to which the energies, resources, and time of a particular school community are focused on teaching and learning is a metric that assesses the health and vibrancy of the culture. While some might think that a majority of the time in a typical school is focused on these domains, sadly that is not always the case. Many minutes and hours are consumed with safety drills, disseminating information about flu vaccines, fundraising drives, compliance issues, PTO announcements, answering emails, transportation matters, and a range of maintenance responsibilities. While these activities are valuable endeavors that are related tangentially to our larger goals, tasks of this kind have taken up an increasingly higher percentage of the limited time that educators have to instruct and collaborate. In shaping a culture, a leader must minimize the many distractions that draw attention and energy away from teaching and learning. At the same time, this leader must utilize the potential of every forum, meeting, and conversation to enhance knowledge, strengthen pedagogical skills, and move the school toward higher achievement for all students.

Lesson TWO

"Don't believe everything you think." Thomas E. Kida

In the world of mathematics, complex and powerful theorems rest upon a few key assumptions. Careful logic and thinking builds upon core assumptions to create helpful applications or theorems. In the world of school, many of the behaviors of teachers and administrators that influence learning rest upon a few key assumptions or beliefs that are held about intelligence and what it means to be smart. However, these assumptions are often invisible and rarely, if ever, discussed, studied, or adapted. One of the important tasks of leadership involves uncovering these often-camouflaged assumptions so that the underlying forces influencing learning within the environment can be understood and altered if necessary. I owe a great debt to social psychologist Carol Dweck for her decades of research that uncovered these powerful cognitive influences that impact learners.

Develop and promote new mindsets about learning

These forces can affect achievement in several ways including the extent to which students and staff will persevere when faced with difficulty. They also impact the responses that teachers and students will have to their mistakes and setbacks. The link between these forces and underlying beliefs about intelligence is not well understood. Once beliefs about learning are examined and unwrapped, educators can better understand some of the root causes of underachievement and poor academic and study skills.

A powerful example of how beliefs can impact achievement is found in the changes that have taken place over the past four decades in women's sports. Watching the U.S. Women's Basketball team win the gold medal in Beijing brought back memories of when we used to believe that women could not play sports as well as men. Prior to the Title IX rule changes that were implemented in 1972, a women's basketball team consisted of six players, not five. Players were only allowed to dribble twice before passing and only certain players, called rovers, were allowed to cross the half court line and run the full length of the court.

Why did these different rules for female athletes exist? Why were our beliefs limited in regard to athletics and women's capacities? Anyone old enough to remember watching women play this diluted game of basketball might also remember that these rules reinforced prevailing beliefs about women's inability to be athletic and competitive. With Title IX and a shift in cultural norms, athletic rule changes forced an alteration in prevailing assumptions. Women gained access to skillful coaching, improved practice conditions, and higher expectations. A limiting set of beliefs was exchanged for a more liberating set of assumptions, which led to the rapid development and improved achievement of women in sports.

What beliefs might be limiting the development of students today? Schools are fertile grounds for beliefs about intellectual capacity. Could we possibly see, for example, a change in our mathematics achievement if we explored and changed our perceptions about who can do math? There seems to be an unspoken belief that when it comes to mathematics, "some people have it, while others don't." Would our schools, our curricula, and our grouping patterns look different if we believed that the overwhelming majority of our students have the capacity to think mathematically?

Limiting beliefs about intelligence
- Intelligence is fixed.
- Only the few bright children can achieve at a high level.
- Speed is what counts. Faster is smarter.
- Inborn intelligence is the determinant of success.
- Mistakes are a sign of weakness.
- Smart students work independently.

Saphier and D'Auria

> **Liberating beliefs about intelligence**
> - Intelligence is malleable.
> - All children are capable of high achievement, not just the fastest and most confident.
> - You are not supposed to understand everything the first time around.
> - Consistent effort is the main determinant of success.
> - Mistakes help one learn.
> - Smart students seek out assistance, resources, and alternative pathways.
>
> *Saphier and D'Auria*

LIMITING AND LIBERATING BELIEFS ABOUT LEARNING

Many schools are characterized by their limiting beliefs about children's intelligence. Schools with powerful cultures are distinguished by the liberating beliefs they hold about what it means to be smart. One example of a limiting belief is "faster is smarter." An incredibly common belief that has deep roots in our society and in our schools holds that "bright" students are "quick" in their thinking or "fast learners." Those who are not considered as smart or less intelligent are considered "slow." Young students learn early in their school career that they want to be "first" in line, first to be done with a task, and even "first to tell Grandma."

It is not unusual for students to put their pencils down noisily when they finish a test, subtly signaling that the students who are done first are very smart. While there is deep acceptance of these ideas, they carry significant burdens for the learner. As students mature, many will conclude that they are, for example, "not good at math or reading" if they are not "quick" at it. Students often believe that they must learn things "first time around." If they need more time or don't "get it right away," they fear they will be considered stupid.

Lillian Katz, an international leader in early childhood education, shared a story that illuminates the limiting power of this belief. She describes receiving a phone call late one night from her son who was struggling in his first year of teaching. She picked up the phone with some alarm and said, "What's the matter?" "Mom," he said, "You speak to educators all across the world. How about giving me some help?" Ms. Katz thought for a while and said, "No matter what age children you teach, whether they be little kids or big kids, teach your students to pull on your pant leg if they are small, or raise their hands if they are middle sized kids, or come up to your desk after class if they are bigger, and say, 'I didn't understand, could you go over that again? Can you please review that one more time?'" There was silence on the other end of the phone for a while and Ms. Katz was worried that perhaps her son had nodded off while she was talking. Then her son spoke and said, "Why didn't anyone tell me that when I was in second grade? Why did I think all this time that I was supposed to understand the first time?"

The idea that one is supposed to understand "the first time around" hit home for me a few years ago when I became intrigued in the science behind DNA. I was in an airport lounge and noticed that DNA was the lead topic in the current issue of Scientific American. I was excited to teach myself about this intriguing theme. After reading the article, I had a sinking feeling. My understanding had not grown appreciably as a result of my reading. The next day at school I ran into the science department chair, Bill Atherton. I had come to admire Bill for his outstanding teaching skills and his deep knowledge and love of science. I told him how excited I was to read about DNA in the current issue of his favorite magazine. I explained that I was disappointed that the article did not appreciably enhance my understanding of the topic. I was bowled over by how Bill replied. He asked, "How many times did you read it?" I replied, "Once." Bill then went on to say, "Well, no wonder you didn't understand it. I have never understood one of those articles from reading them once. Sometimes I have to read them three or four times." I immediately felt like Lilian Katz's son. Here I was an experienced educational leader and someone who had been a student for decades. Yet, what Bill Atherton was telling me was almost shocking. This exchange underscored for me how powerful the assumption or belief about "getting it the first time" is embedded in our perspectives about learning.

This belief also surfaced in a discussion I had with the staff when I was a middle school principal. The topic at one of our faculty meetings was a review of our test retake policy. I asked the staff how many of them would allow a retake on an exam that a student had failed. About half of the teachers raised their hands. I then asked those teachers what students had to do in order to earn the chance to re-take the exam. For some, it was attending after school sessions. For others, it was completing a packet on the main concepts and skills of the unit. For a few, students had to re-study the material in a self-directed manner.

I then asked the teachers who would allow students to retake an exam what final grade they would give a student for a unit test. If, for example, the student earned a score of 50 on the first exam and took the second exam and earned a 100, what would be the recorded grade for the test? Not a single teacher indicated that he or she would record "100" as the score for the test. Some stated that they would average the two grades; others suggested that they would have to adjust the average if it exceeded the top score that a retake could earn; still others would employ a complicated mathematical formula involving multiple factors. I asked the teachers the thinking behind their practice. Teachers responded that they felt that giving students more time on a test was an equity problem and would encourage laziness. Students would not study for the material at the time of the first test, knowing they could easily take a second test. Most importantly, for many teachers it just felt unfair.

While there is some logic to the teachers' concerns, this commonly held perspective contributes to an environment in which understanding becomes secondary to knowing quickly. And while some would argue that this is the way the world works, it is also clear that mastering challenging material requires lots of study, repeated practice, and constant research and review. More importantly, linking being really smart to "getting it" quickly can be potentially very damaging. When a student who has been successful encounters, for the first time, a subject or a concept that he or she does not "get quickly," it is not unusual for the student to withdraw, give up, and conclude that he or she is not smart in this area.

We face this challenge in schools because not only do many students need more time and practice but so do many teachers and administrators. The concepts and content that we want teachers and administrators to learn are often challenging and complex. Teachers and administrators also need study, practice, research, and review to learn the skills of improving school culture and keeping seventh graders engaged while they are taught about absolute value.

SCHOOLS AS PAINFUL PLACES

The prevailing beliefs and assumptions we have about intelligence not only limit learning, they also contribute to making schools painful places for students. Kirsten Olson, a visiting professor of education at Wheaton College, addressed this concern in her article, "The Wounds of Schooling." For the past decade, Olson has been interviewing people to chronicle their "learning histories." She asks them to recall their earliest school memories, describe their most powerful learning experiences, and discuss the perceived relationship between pleasurable learning and schooling. For many people, this connection is a negative one. In these interviews, adults often discuss painful recollections that have endured through multiple decades. They vividly describe negative comments by teachers, social issues with their peers, and their fear of being shamed for poor performance.

While an education can be an incredible gift, it can also leave painful scars. Olson notes that:

> *The process of schooling, while providing market-pleasing attainments, has diffuse psychological effects for many. It can make us risk-averse or cause us to underestimate ourselves. We may be overly obedient to authority, toxically rebellious, or simply deadened. We may have suppressed creativity and lost the habit of thinking novelly from too many standardized assessments. We are wounded and we don't know why.*

Olson describes several factors that contribute to the negative impact of schooling. While Olson believes that learning often involves "intuition, risk, and ambiguity," she views as damaging the notion that learning is a product that can be acquired in predictable stages and carefully measured by testing.

Another critical factor identified by Olson as contributing to school-inflicted wounds is "our truncated notion of ability." She writes that "We are also hobbled by our underdeveloped, too-simple ideas about human ability." Our ideas about intelligence, formed in the early 20th Century to sort students with efficiency, tend to construct ability as something innate, fixed at birth, and easily measured. An ever-growing body of cognitive research in America and in other highly successful cultures is discrediting this long-held assumption. It is demonstrating that effort is the most crucial component of academic achievement. American schools, however, have been very slow to alter the DNA of beliefs about ability. Our ideas about inborn, unchanging capacity in students tend to live on, making grades and test scores, even in very young children, highly public evaluations of ability and worth. Students themselves often internalize these views in ways that affect them for life.

When students are liberated from limiting beliefs about ability and genuinely become engaged in learning, it is an incredibly exciting and beautiful sight. Figuring out how we can both capture and initiate this passion is one of the fundamental challenges of teaching. Often the solution does not come in predictable and typical ways. An experience on a football team, a connection with an after school club, a recommended book, a casual "off-topic" conversation in a classroom, a note of appreciation or interest from a coach or teacher, or a few minutes playing with a computer game can lead to a question, an insight, a sense of curiosity. Years later, a successful career or an important change in one's life can often be traced back to one of these magical moments.

In our attempts to improve education in this country, I wish we could spend more energy and research dollars understanding how powerful learning is inspired, nurtured, and sustained. Our efforts so far with national education reform have led to some improved test scores and more standardization. Too few of our efforts are aimed at creating an environment that substitutes the current message of "Learn or we will hurt you." for "Learn, or you will hurt yourself."

CHILDREN'S BELIEFS ABOUT INTELLIGENCE

Carol Dweck, researcher and professor of psychology, has studied the way students respond to setbacks and failures. In her early research, she studied students who had an equivalent skill level as measured by standardized tests. Dweck's research revealed that the beliefs that students hold about intelligence can be divided into two major frameworks or what she describes as mindsets. One framework is a growth mindset and the other is a fixed mindset. Dweck's research on individual perceptions of intelligence shows that there are significant achievement gains over time for those students who believe intelligence is not a fixed entity but rather is malleable. Malleable intelligence is a cornerstone of a growth mindset.

There are substantial differences in the type of goals that students with a growth mindset set for themselves. They use different strategies to achieve success and take a different perspective on their setbacks and mistakes. Youngsters who believe their intelligence is a fixed trait tend to seek out only positive evaluations of their abilities. These students are focused more on how others will judge their ability than on learning or mastering a skill. They are apt to become discouraged in the face of setbacks and see failure as an indictment of their abilities. These setbacks equate to having not enough ability. In contrast, young people who view their intelligence as malleable tend to pursue goals that increase their abilities. They focus more on learning outcomes and less on how well they performed. These students remain confident in the face of obstacles because they tend to see impediments as a normal and expected part of the learning process. They believe that working hard will result in improving their ability.

My middle school administrative team and I worked continually to have our students understand that coming after class to see a teacher for extra help was not a sign that they were "dumb." In fact, the reality was just the opposite. The students who regularly worked with their teachers before or after school were often the ones attaining the highest grades.

There are two assumptions or beliefs that are commonly held by students and influence them to behave in ways that obstruct achievement:

- Students should not work too hard because this amount of effort signals that they do not have a lot of brain power.
- Students have to "get it quickly" or else be viewed as "slow."

Because of these assumptions, we can begin to understand why so many students spend enormous amounts of time and energy avoiding their "weaknesses." They will work on the areas in which they are already strong and avoid areas that need strengthening. They view the act of going for help after school as an indictment of their lack of intelligence. It is also not uncommon to find, for example, that when students do their homework, they work first on the assignment or content area in which they feel most confident. The strong reader might avoid the math problems. The math "person" might avoid the reading he found challenging.

It is astonishing for this experienced educator to realize that, for many students, schools are places to get better in areas in which they are already confident. How do we help educators change the prevailing school environment in which students avoid working hard in order to not look dumb and focus primarily on areas in which they are already relatively strong?

ADULTS' BELIEFS ABOUT INTELLIGENCE

One way to change this climate is to lead faculty to explore their beliefs and assumptions about intelligence. We know that the assumptions adults in schools hold about intelligence influence many aspects of their practice:

- How they group students for instruction
- The level of expectations they communicate for students
- How they respond to their own errors and mistakes as teachers
- How long they will persist with their students who don't understand a concept the first time it is taught

The dominant belief that innate ability trumps effort and strategies runs very deep in our society. When I was growing up in New York, my friends would ask, "Who is the smartest in your family?" I would respond, "My brother is. I have to work hard for my grades." This distinction between "smart" and "working hard" was not a peculiar notion that resided only in my mind. We consistently see examples of how ability, talent, and what Dweck refers to as the notion of being a "natural" are qualities that are greatly admired. While sometimes adults preach the benefits of effort, our actions speak much louder than our words.

The following story underscores this dissonance between what adults say and how we behave.

> *I was selected to coach a Little League team in my hometown. I had 15 ten-year old boys on my team. I was excited to coach them and I called each of them on the phone to share my enthusiasm and to tell them when we would have our first practice. At our first meeting, I shared my hopes and dreams for our "great team." I talked about the importance of effort and teamwork. We got on the field and I hit the players some ground balls, some fly balls, and had each of them take a turn hitting and pitching. At the end of practice, I knew who the "stars" of the team would be and who would be "holding up the rear." I continued to preach the importance of working hard and supporting one another. After a couple of weeks of practice, it was time for our first game and I had a problem. I could only put nine players out in the field and six had to sit on the bench. I placed my nine best players out in the field. There is a mandatory "two-inning" rule in our town's Little League. Each of the bench players was put in for those mandatory two innings. As many coaches know, right field is the place to hide weaker players and that is where I placed my bench players. While I was preaching the importance of effort and teamwork, with this strategy I was teaching my players that what I really valued was talent. In fact, I am embarrassed to report that some of the "bench players" quickly figured out that if they did not show up, the team would do better because I would not have to put them in for their innings. Not surprisingly, at the end of the season those players who experienced more playing time improved while those players who had fewer opportunities to get on the field and bat did not. The biggest learning for my players, sadly, was that achievement is linked more to talent than it is to effort.*

LIMITING AND LIBERATING BELIEFS ABOUT TEACHING

The learning and beliefs that govern what it means to be intelligent abound in school environments and yet rarely are these beliefs raised to the conscious level so that they can be examined and altered if necessary. One task of leaders is to probe for the hidden beliefs. These assumptions have significant influence on our ultimate work: creating smarter students. Schools, like other complex organizations, are systems and very interrelated. The beliefs about learning that impact students are linked to and impact the adults in schools. It is not unusual to find that in schools in which students are judged partially by how quickly they learn, the adults will shy away from work that requires slow and careful learning over time. In these schools, teachers who do not master technology quickly might find ways to avoid using technology. The administrators will offer one-day workshops to introduce a complex strategy, such as differentiated instruction, rather than investing in more in-depth work that teachers will need to genuinely and effectively incorporate a new pedagogical approach into their teaching repertoire.

It is educators' fixed beliefs about themselves as learners, not their ability, that can keep them from improving. Imagine if all the educators in a district believed that regardless of the native ability they brought to learning technology, or lesson design, or working with autistic students, they could improve their practice, expand their repertoire, and become more effective. Educators with these beliefs would evidence less resistance and reluctance. They would embrace professional growth with a sense of excitement, interest, and enthusiasm.

The mindset of educators influences what they will or will not do when they encounter students who do not learn after receiving an initial round of instruction. As Becky and Rick DuFour acknowledge, the mark of a school ultimately is what happens when students do not learn. From my observations, the response of teachers to unsuccessful learning in their students often flows from the teacher's views on intelligence. Too often, teachers attribute student failure to a lack of "natural" ability or they blame failure on the lack of parental support. In contrast, educators who hold more liberating views about intelligence, or Dweck's "growth mindset," will seek out different pedagogical approaches. They also will influence students to alter their strategies and apply more effort in the face of obstructed learning.

It is my contention that if teachers believe their abilities are malleable, they are more likely to view the abilities of their students in a similar manner. A "growth mindset" can inoculate a school community against the defeatism that can easily overtake a taxed system. The role of educational leaders is to help adults and students examine their beliefs about intelligence with the goal of motivating themselves and their students to redouble their efforts and experiment with strategies for success.

A REVISED DEFINITION OF "SMART" FOR STUDENTS AND EDUCATORS

As we examine liberating mindsets for teachers and students, we must define "smart" because the ultimate mission of schools is to develop smarter students. Without an explicit and common understanding of what we mean by smart, we run the risk of assuming all educators share a common perspective of what it means to be smart. Unfortunately, with today's heavy emphasis on test scores, we also run the risk of seeing smartness as defined by levels of performance on a test.

While there is a correlation between intelligence and certain tests, test data offers a very narrow view of educational achievement when it is compared to the complex mission of schools. Based on the work of Dweck and the experiences of many teachers, administrators, and students, I would like to offer an alternative to what it means to be smart that is less static. This definition is connected more to what people do than how they are. Intelligence, in this view, is not a permanent condition; it is possible at any moment to act or not act smartly.

LESSON TWO

> **WHAT SMART STUDENTS, TEACHERS, ADMINISTRATORS DO**
> *(The Growth Mindset)*
>
> They ask themselves when they face a challenge:
> **How do I do this?**
> not
> Can I do this?
>
> **They realize that mistakes are part of learning.**
> Mistakes are not a sign of weakness.
>
> **They increase their efforts as things get more difficult.**
> They don't give up.
>
> In the face of complications and problems:
> **They seek out different and better strategies.**
> They do not stick with a strategy that is not working.
>
> *Adapted from Dweck*

We live in an era that has heavily emphasized the importance of test scores. It is no small feat, therefore, to develop a school climate that does not shy away from high achievement and that does emphasize broader skills and different ways of measuring achievement. I worry that somehow the scores on these high stakes tests will be seen as accurately describing academic progress in all the areas that are essential to a good education. While data from these exams can provide parents and teachers with an important lens for viewing how students are developing in several academic areas, they provide very little information about how persistent, curious, reflective, or creative a student might be. It is all of these qualities that are extremely important to students' future success.

Being well educated involves possessing a complex set of characteristics. It is difficult to attach a single number to such a quality. We have little patience these days with characteristics that cannot be easily quantified. Quantification makes it easier to compare, rank, and draw logical conclusions, but no one number about a student accurately represents the intricate set of factors it is intended to summarize.

Equating a numerical value with an elaborate array of attributes and characteristics is not a new idea. At the turn of the century, psychologists and other scientists became intrigued with tests for assessing human intelligence. The scores on tests developed and administered by men like Alfred Binet and H.H. Goddard helped reduce the mysterious phenomenon of human intelligence into a simple number known as the IQ. Despite the rigor and objectivity that researchers worked hard to bring to their studies on intelligence, it was difficult to subtract biases and hidden assumptions. As a case in point, significant studies concluded that more than 80% of immigrants tested were feeble-minded. R.M. Yerkes and E.G. Boring, who helped shape the intelligence testing of 1.75 million recruits during World War I, concluded that the average mental age of white American adults stood just above the edge of moronity and that the darker peoples of southern Europe were less intelligent than their fairer-skinned northern neighbors. Despite significant violations in the testing protocol and the fact that many of the recruits had never before held a pencil or taken a test, "scientific" conclusions were derived from the data. For example, a considerable number of the men who took the test scored a zero. Regardless of the fact that testers considered the large number of zeros to be an indication of misunderstood or poorly delivered instructions, Boring concluded that zero scores came from men who were too stupid to successfully complete any of the test items. Interestingly, Yerkes found a relationship between intelligence and the amount of schooling. Yet when trying to explain why northern test takers scored higher than some test takers from the south, instead of suggesting that the difference was linked to the fact that northern subjects attended several more years of school, Yerkes and his associates argued that economic and social factors attracted the more intelligent southerner to the north.

Eighty years later, we are again in the middle of a significant testing era. High stakes tests have been established across fifty states. I appreciate the value of improving our schools and instituting universally applied high standards, but I am skeptical about what all the numbers mean. Learning and understanding are obviously affected by skillful teaching, rich curricula, and high expectations.

However, familiarity with the English language and American culture, financial resources, and safe school environments are just a few of the other factors that can influence student learning and impact assessment scores. Recent statewide testing results do not differ greatly from a ranking of communities by socio-economic factors. Charts that evaluate communities by these scores can blind us to the problems and challenges that many school systems face. They make it easy to dismiss the potential of the students in these schools, some of whom are our newest immigrants or the daughters and sons of families with extremely limited resources.

And what is our responsibility and that of our children to help close the gap between the richest and the poorest in our states? Shouldn't our knowledge of math, science, and social studies be partially gauged by how we apply our awareness to strengthen and improve society? Do high scores mean that students will successfully contribute to their communities and help achieve a more equitable society? Do low scores mean there is little hope that some invention, work of art, or loving family might emerge from the work of these future adults? It is out of this growing skepticism about testing data that some colleges are beginning to ignore SAT scores.

Given that my father could have been one of those southern European "feeble-minded" immigrants who came to this country, I tend to view with skepticism the capability of a test to capture the complexity and potential of the mind when it acts in concert with the human spirit. We have too many recent examples of smart people doing stupid things. One day we might learn that our achievements are not a function of a standardized score but how we react and respond to a set of circumstances. The measures I have come to value are how we think, how we act, how hard we work, how much we persevere, and how much we contribute to our children, our families, our communities, and our country.

Lesson THREE

"Effectiveness without values is a tool without a purpose." Edward de Bono

Core values answer the question, "What does this school or organization stand for?" While core values are not a requirement, they do make a difference. When they are genuinely incorporated into the daily life and routines of an organization, they provide a means to gain focus, clarity, and collective strength. They separate good organizations from mediocre ones. The impact of core values can be detected when similar organizations are compared. It is often because of the values that are embedded in an organization that it stands out in a positive way.

Cultivate core values

Schools that value caring and supportive human relationships, as one example, understand that how people are treated can either enhance or diminish the vitality of a school culture and its productivity. I have seen schools that give lip service to this core value. These schools may open and close on time and organize effectively for their students. However, they may do little to inspire reflection on what it means to be a respectful, inclusive community. In other schools in which caring and supportive human relationships is an actively implemented core value, decisions and actions in the schools are guided by this value. This core value positively impacts the attitude of secretaries who greet parents, the communication between parents and teachers, and interactions between students and the adults in the school. As a result, each constituency in the school feels respected and valued. Adults and students in these schools are willing to work hard and demonstrate their commitment to the mission of the school. In my experience, these seemingly little bits add up to significant and powerful differences that help to distinguish healthy school cultures from those that are ailing.

Core values are, on one hand, amorphous qualities easily dealt with in a superficial way or not acted upon at all. On the other hand, when taken seriously and done well, they establish a challenging but rewarding framework for a school community. Schools can function without core values. However, when core values are present a school gains a rudder to guide its decision making when competing needs and multiple demands press upon it.

KNOWLEDGE IS POWER IN JOHNSON CITY

Al Mamary, former Superintendent of Schools for Johnson City, New York, demonstrated effective leadership in his Outcomes Based Approach to Education that was launched in 1972. Johnson City, at the time, was a lower middle-class community with few professional citizens and the second highest poverty rate of 10 urban districts in its county. Over 20% of its school population qualified for free or reduced-price lunch. The district had a sizable Asian immigrant population with limited English proficiency. In 1972, Johnson City ranked 14th out of 14 districts in its county on academic achievement as measured on standardized tests. Approximately 45 to 50% of its students scored at or above grade level in reading and math in grades 1 through 8. By 1977, the percentages rose to about 70% and by 1984 they ranged between 80 and 90%.

When Ronald Brandt interviewed Al Mamary about the positive and significant impact of his leadership, Mamary shared one of his core values - knowledge is power. "A position in this district is not power. Instead…knowledge is power, using knowledge is power…We are all co-workers, and co-learners and co-doers. And I think that is why the district is where it is today." Mamary not only espoused this value he brought it to life by the way decisions were made in the district. Mamary consistently strove for 100% agreement about important decisions even if that meant returning to discuss an issue many, many times. The notion that real change does not occur from a position of power but rather from the power that comes from learning is extremely potent. Mamary was willing to devote hours to educating his staff about the important teaching and learning issues for which he was seeking their support. This value – knowledge is power - had a significant impact on the culture of the Johnson City schools. They became a work environment in which it was safe to learn, to question, and to debate.

LUNCHROOM LESSONS

As a middle school principal, I worked with the staff to develop our school's core values. Three values that emerged from our work were respect for both people and property, responsibility for one's actions, and the importance of recycling mistakes into learning opportunities. Once the values had been established, a small subcommittee worked with me to resolve a difficult problem in the school related to lunchroom behavior. Our goal was to ameliorate the problem and to use our newly established values to guide our work. The values provided a target for how we wanted students to behave.

The school did not have access to any recess area or fields so energetic middle-school students spent their entire lunch period in the cafeteria. While this situation posed its own challenges, equally difficult for the lunch supervisors was getting students to clean up after themselves. The school was large, with each lunch shift serving approximately 350 students. Understandably, many of the lunch supervisors did not know the students' names. Adding to the problem, the food services department was an independent operation that daily sold a small number of purchased lunches. In order to stay in the black, they provided a few popular "a la carte" items that were loaded with sugar. Many teachers complained about how "hyper" students became after leaving the cafeteria. The most concerning aspect of our lunchroom problem, however, was what teachers referred to as "MIA's"-students missing in action. If, for example, fifteen students were absent in the 7th grade on a given day, a quick count of the students at lunch may show that as many as twenty-five students were "missing." When we went to look for the "missing," we found some in the nurse's office complaining of stomachaches. A few were hiding in the bathrooms and others were in line to purchase a la carte items and wandered the café without ever taking a seat. A by-product of this analysis was the realization that one of the most challenging aspects of middle school life was finding a place to sit in the cafeteria. For a number of students, this challenge was anxiety producing. They could take a seat at an empty table, but that might entail being labeled a social failure. They could risk sitting at a table where more "popular kids" sat, but that might lead to hearing some hurtful comments.

This examination of our café led the committee to realize that our core values were not alive and well during lunchtime. Students did not feel respected. Lunchtime was an indicator of how non-inclusive and non-welcoming our school community was. Additionally, our students did not have a commitment to the school that resulted in their cleaning up after themselves. As the problem became clearer, the committee's thinking moved toward trying to address the anonymity of the students. Because lunch supervisors did not know the names of students, they were at a distinct disadvantage as they asked students to follow the rules and meet their responsibilities. Consequently, one of the strategies the committee started to examine was assigning seats in the café. Staff thought that assigned seats would help ameliorate the isolation and the daily risk involved in "finding a seat." As the idea of assigned seats emerged at one meeting, it became clear that some of the members felt anxious about this proposal. Committee members worried that assigning seats would be a drastic change from past practice. Additionally, parents had often been told by school officials that because there was no recess, students could socialize during lunchtime by sitting with their friends from elementary school.

As the discussion unfolded, I sensed in the committee something I also saw from time to time in students – fear of making a mistake. While we were trying to brainstorm ways to strengthen respect in the café, we almost missed an opportunity to take a risk, create a new set of expectations, and make adjustments from what we learned from our experiment. Committee members expressed their concerns about angry parents, angry students, and staff resistance because it would be they who would ultimately have to enforce the new rules. However, guided by the idea that learning from our mistakes was a value we wanted to embrace, the committee forged ahead with its improvement plan. We did not achieve instant success in the cafeteria. Over a period of two years, however, the cafeteria problems were significantly diminished. Students no longer had to worry about finding a seat. There were no longer isolated students sitting at tables. Students' behavior improved because our middle schoolers took responsibility for cleaning their own areas, which allowed each class to enter an inviting lunchroom. While many factors contributed to these positive developments, paying attention to our values at a very critical time helped to give us direction and confidence.

LESSON THREE

RESPECT IN THE CLASSROOM

While values are developed by many schools, it has been my experience that they are often forgotten after an initial period of promulgation. It is a leader's responsibility to breathe life continually into the values and help others to remember their importance by taking every opportunity to use them as a guide. A teacher in my district was upset with a student who acted inappropriately in a classroom setting. The teacher felt that the misbehavior was significant enough to involve the vice principal. When the vice principal investigated, he discovered that the student was distressed by a comment from the teacher after he had asked a question that the teacher felt was inappropriate. The teacher, in front of the class, described the student's question as "ignorant."

This situation can be viewed from several perspectives – consequences for the students' poor behavior, appropriateness of the teacher's response to the student's conduct, and adherence by both parties to the core value of respect. While it is always appropriate for students to ask and teachers to provide feedback to students about their questioning, students and teachers are expected to adhere to the values that are espoused by the district. This vignette reinforces how core values can inform a conversation and contribute an additional lens through which to view and understand a situation. It also demonstrates that the ultimate benefit of core values is to impact the work environment and enhance the climate within the district. The challenges that schools face are often ill structured problems whose solutions require decisions formed by a combination of insight, analysis, and values. Empirical analysis alone will not provide a definitive answer to most problems.

Schools continually are confronted with difficult decisions. Selecting the school system's approach to the instruction of reading and writing, for example, requires thoughtful review of research combined with an assessment of the needs of students. However, this kind of thinking, while necessary, is not sufficient. It is rare that a single program would emerge from this kind of analysis. Rather, a variety of strong possibilities might emerge. In order to make a final selection, these potential programmatic solutions will have to be examined through a set of value lenses that ask:

- What can the system afford?
- What is the relative importance of this initiative compared to other district priorities?
- Who will make the final decision on academic programs and how will it be made?
- How well is the diversity of the student body reflected in curriculum materials?

In a place like Johnson City, the collaborative process that Al Mamary valued might result in an approach different from that of a nearby system with similar needs, access to the same research studies, but a different level of respect for collaborative decision making. Core values guide decision-making, channel limited resources to district priorities, shape the norms of every day behavior, and consequently, have significant influence on school culture.

Core values, when they are genuinely present in the life of a school community, help students to learn important principles about life. These principles are as important to learn as the math and literacy skills and concepts we teach. Just because we have not devised a standardized test to assess how well our students internalize core values does not mean they may not be extremely important in students' lives in the future. In 2009, decisions and behaviors from Wall Street businessmen led our nation to a near financial collapse. I have little doubt that the business leaders who were involved in the financial meltdown were smart and successful learners in school. They have demonstrated competence in the skills and concepts that we test and that we promote as critical to the educational future of our country. Despite their academic prowess, these leaders lacked the values that put the common good before their individual benefit.

LESSON THREE

Schools have a responsibility not only to teach skills and concepts but to nurture and strengthen values. A school community that has developed and embraced core values helps to teach important societal principles such as respect for human differences and the importance of compassion for the vitality of our communities.

Haim Ginott, author and psychologist, was also a school principal. In this role, he wrote the following to his staff:

Dear Teachers:

I am a survivor of a concentration camp. My eyes saw what no person should witness. Gas chambers built by learned engineers. Children poisoned by educated physicians. Infants killed by trained nurses. Women and babies shot and burned by high school and college graduates.

So I am suspicious of education. My request is: help your students become more human. Your efforts must never produce learned monsters, skilled psychopaths, or educated Eichmanns. Reading, writing, and arithmetic are important only if they serve to make our children more human.

Haim Ginott

Lesson FOUR

"Learning is a social activity. We humans learn primarily from one another. Listening closely to what someone has to say reveals novel ideas that cement a friendship or grow a business. Listening builds confidence and trust — the cornerstones of every work relationship." Roland Barth

Positive, professional relationships provide the energy and fuel that move a school forward. When these relationships falter, so do the chances that a learning community can find the time and dedication to strive for ambitious goals and continuous improvement. While a great deal has been written about curriculum, instruction, and assessment, what has not been sufficiently documented is the fact that interactions between and among adults in a school absorb an incredible amount of the time and energy available for work. Leaders learn that an important responsibility of leadership is learning the art and skills needed to develop, maintain, and nurture professional relationships.

The term relationships might evoke images of people getting along, knowing each other well, and caring for one another during tough times. While these attributes are important and valued by teachers, they represent necessary but not sufficient conditions. The challenges that schools face are complex.

Teaching students with a wide spectrum of cognitive, emotional, and social needs requires ongoing collaboration and teamwork among specialists, classroom teachers, and administrators. There often will not be unanimity as different strategic interventions are discussed and analyses are formed. In order to optimize resources and insure that our best thinking is applied to meet student needs, it is critical that the quality of relationships that exist among staff members can sustain honest dialogue, philosophical clashes, and heated debate. Because most schools are not resource abundant, the ability to meet the ambitious goals of a school community will be reduced significantly if the staff

Professional relationships are the engine of change

is not working extraordinarily hard and willing to "go the extra mile." This work ethic and attitude is often supported by high quality professional relationships in which people are very respectful of their colleagues but unabashed in their willingness to disagree agreeably.

It is essential for leaders to understand that the quality of the relationships among the staff is both a gauge of the health of the culture and a key component for insuring that a school is continually improving and meeting the changing needs of its students. The quality of relationships provides one of the most significant levers of change. Michael Fullan and his colleagues note that:

> *The single factor common to successful change is that relationships improve. If relationships improve, schools get better. If relationships remain the same or get worse, ground is lost. Thus, building relationships with diverse people and groups – especially with people who think differently – is a must.*

Managing these relationships is an important part of keeping a school moving forward. Many new administrators are shocked by how much time they spend untangling the problems that emerge among the adults in a school. More importantly, new leaders learn quickly that managing conflict is one of the biggest challenges they face. Many new administrators think that the authority that rests within their positions will be sufficient to influence the other adults in their building to change their approach with students or alter their perspective on curriculum and assessment. They quickly find out that one's authority is not something one can use casually or frequently and still maintain one's effectiveness as a leader.

In my work with aspiring principals and department heads, I find myself helping them unlearn this link between power and impact. It is unquestionable that one's power and authority, when embedded in a leadership position, can initiate change. However, power and authority do not have the enduring influence and impact that are derived from high quality, professional relationships. Our ability as leaders to help people change, embrace a new strategy, adopt a new practice, and alter the way they go about their work is linked more deeply to the quality of our relationships with them than to the power we have over them. Power often produces superficial compliance. When thoughtful change is supported by open and honest relationships, the change will be more durable. It will even "stick" when the leader is not around or visible.

Joseph Nye, former Dean of Harvard's Kennedy School of Government, summed up this idea, which he refers to as "soft power," in this way:

> *In the business world, smart executives know that leadership is not just a matter of issuing commands, but also involves leading by example and attracting others to do what you want. It is difficult to run a large organization by commands alone unless you can get others to buy in to your values.*

Nye expands his explanation of the distinction between soft and hard power as follows:

> One way to think about the difference between hard and soft power is to consider the variety of ways you can obtain the outcomes you want:
>
> - You can command me to change my preferences and do what you want by threatening me with force or economic sanctions.
>
> - You can induce me to do what you want by using your economic power to pay me.
>
> - You can restrict my preferences by setting the agenda in such a way that my more extravagant wishes seem too unrealistic to pursue.
>
> - Or you can appeal to my sense of attraction, love or duty **in our relationship,** and appeal to our shared values about the justness of contributing to those shared values and purposes.

Soft power is influence that is based not within the authority of one's position but within a relationship in which values are shared. Effective leadership depends upon developing relationships that create a momentum for continual improvement. There are tools and skills that must be honed in order to insure that the power of relationships is used to move the school forward. These tools and skills also are essential for solving the innumerable problems that arise within a school environment and can detract from the academic focus.

The following skills, which will be examined in the next three lessons, play an important role in helping leaders address the challenges of developing relationships. These skills strengthen leaders' ability to:

1. Courageously address nondiscussables
2. Utilize emotional intelligence
3. Transform difficult conversations into understanding

LESSON FIVE

"There is a prevailing belief that in order to get ahead, we must be cautious in telling the truth. To act courageously is to follow an unpopular path. It means to confront an issue when others are acting as if there is no issue —to say that a meeting is not going well when everyone else seems totally satisfied." Peter Block, *The Empowered Manager*

"Front stabbing is better than backstabbing." Judy Boroscheck, Former Director, Curriculum and Instruction, Wellesley MA Public Schools

Courageously address nondiscussables

A highly regarded article by Roland Barth, "The Culture Builder," claims that the health of a school is inversely proportional to the number of nondiscussables. Barth defines a nondiscussable as something that is talked about frequently but the conversations are so laden with "anxiety and fearfulness that these conversations take place only in the parking lot, the rest rooms, the playground, the car pool, or the dinner table at home. Fear abounds that open discussion of these incendiary issues - at a faculty meeting, for example - will cause a meltdown. The nondiscussable is the elephant in the living room."

OPEN, HONEST COMMUNICATION

Being able to discuss nondiscussables requires a combination of skills and courage. Speaking openly and honestly is far less common in school environments than one might expect. It is almost an exception rather than the norm. Schools are abuzz with discussion about 21st Century skills and the impact of new technologies on teaching and learning. What is often overlooked is a very traditional and basic concept that is rarely evident in modern school settings - honesty. President Obama, in a speech in Cairo where he addressed the Muslim world, described the notion of addressing nondiscussables:

But I am convinced that in order to move forward, we must say openly the things we hold in our hearts, and that too often are said only behind closed doors. There must be a sustained effort to listen to each other; to learn from each other; to respect one another; and to seek common ground. As the Holy Koran tells us, "Be conscious of God and speak always the truth." That is what I will try to do — to speak the truth as best I can, humbled by the task before us, and firm in my belief that the interests we share as human beings are far more powerful than the forces that drive us apart.

As a principal, my first experience with a nondiscussable occurred when a teacher in my building wanted to discuss changing the rules that governed our traditional science fair for sixth graders. For many years, students entered the science fair by completing an individual project. The teacher wanted to allow students to work cooperatively on a science fair project. I called a meeting of all the sixth grade teachers and outlined the recommendation. One person in the group spoke up quickly and authoritatively, taking a stand critical of the proposal. While her argument was sound, I knew that others in the room disagreed with her. However, no one added to the conversation. Because experience had taught me that some teachers struggle to disagree openly with a colleague, especially around philosophy and values, I was not totally surprised that different views and perspectives did not emerge.

At the time I was not sure how to proceed. I asked people to think about this issue and come to our next meeting ready to discuss the proposal. As I was cleaning up after the meeting, I wandered to the windows that overlooked the parking lot. I noticed that the teachers who were in the meeting a few minutes ago were standing in tight knit conversational groups in the parking lot. I could not hear what they were saying from where I was standing. However, watching the body language, I got the strong sense that there was a lot of passion in the discussion and that, more than likely, they were expressing the ideas that should have been shared at the meeting.

At the next meeting, I shared with the group what I observed and my hypotheses about the dynamics I viewed in the parking lot. The smiles and laughter I heard let me know that my theories were fairly accurate. This conversation helped us to "break the ice" and start the conversation about whether or not to modify the science fair rules. The nondiscussable in this case centered on some teachers' feelings that one of their colleagues, whom they considered a loud mouth, made it difficult for others to contribute at meetings. Another nondiscussable was that staff did not feel comfortable disagreeing with colleagues openly at meetings. By using some humor to acknowledge the "elephant in the room," some of the obstacles that had previously blocked this discussion were removed.

Over the course of several months, the staff engaged in more open and honest dialogue that resulted in changing the ground rules for the science fair. In this climate, the staff was able to wrestle more vigorously with the competing ideas that their colleagues brought to the table. Good ideas had been present in the room all along. However, it was not possible for all members to hear them until we addressed the communication block that had little to do with either science or pedagogy.

Simply acknowledging a nondiscussable can help reduce some of the resistance and anxiety that limits these topics to backdoor channels – like parking lots. While acknowledgment of the nondiscussable helps, it is often important to use strategies that help to create an atmosphere in which people are willing to talk openly.

I consulted on "open and honest communication" in one district in which it became clear that a new professional development (PD) initiative organized by central office had become a nondiscussable. In order to move the PD conversation forward, I divided the room of administrators into two randomly selected groups. I asked the first group to list all the positive impacts of the new PD initiative. The other group was assigned the task of generating all the concerns and difficulties that resulted from the deployment of this initiative. By assigning people randomly to these tasks, I was able to relieve individual administrators of the anxieties that can obstruct honesty. Administrators will find that this strategy and others can help to create a culture in which honest dialogue is more the routine than the exception.

NONDISCUSSABLE TOPICS

When I ask aspiring administrators to make a list of the nondiscussables in their school environments, they find it easy to generate a fairly lengthy list of hot-button topics that are rarely discussed openly. They also have many ideas about why there are so many nondiscussables in schools and the factors that contribute to their not being discussed.

Hot Button Topics

- Teachers who do not pull their weight
- Someone who is a bully at meetings
- Faculty cliques
- Teachers who get favored treatment from an administrator
- Racist staff members
- The incompetence of a leader
- The "brashness" of a new teacher
- The "stodginess" of a veteran teacher
- The ineffectiveness of faculty meetings

Reasons for Nondiscussables

- Institutional inertia
- Fear of retribution
- Lack of sufficient time
- Denial
- Lack of trust
- Fear of damaging a relationship
- Poor leadership
- Fear of responsibility
- The old boys' club
- "Go along to get along"

Why are nondiscussables so prevalent? Is it simply that administrators are insensitive and turn a deaf ear to these charged issues? Are they simply unaware of them? I don't believe either of those reasons describes the actual obstacles to openly discussing charged topics in schools. Nondiscussables are like family secrets. All parties are aware of them. No one feels competent to bring the secret up in a manner that does not unleash pain, anger, or emotional chaos. In order to learn how to bring nondiscussables into the open, leaders have to spend time exploring two personal arenas: their confidence in handling conflict and their ability to manage emotions.

While leadership requires many skills, learning how to manage conflict effectively is central to the work of any leader. There are inevitable conflicts between parents and educators around program delivery for a particular student. There are philosophical conflicts among and between educators. Typically, high schools and middle schools in the same district are at odds on the approaches that best serve students. Similarly, veteran and newer teachers often will disagree on approaches to problems.

D'Auria and King comment:

> *It is our perspective that leadership is ultimately about managing conflict effectively. We think the most helpful way is to create a climate in which honest conversations can occur about what is on people's minds. This climate needs to tolerate a variance in perspectives that flows from diverse values and perceptions. Skillful leaders approach problems and dilemmas by assuming that their perspective alone does not provide sufficient information to make effective decisions. Consequently, effective leaders seek out different opinions and, if the climate is healthy, people will actually share what they think. The belief that lies behind this approach is the notion that "none of us is as smart as all of us." The means of accomplishing this goal is through the building of healthy, professional relationships.*

D'Auria and King go on to point out that while school leaders, like all leaders, must manage conflict, educators are sometimes the least prepared for this task.

> *Let's begin by pointing out that just about all school administrators begin their careers as teachers or guidance counselors. And when young adults choose to become teachers they tend to do so for value-driven reasons: to influence the next generation, to communicate a love for a discipline, to work with children or adolescents, and to be part of a collegial community. We are going to go out on a limb: educators tend to be nice people. We value relationships, especially with students, above all else. And in sharp contrast with people who chose professions in business or the law, we tend to be conflict-aversive.*
>
> *One of the great mysteries of our profession is why so little is done to prepare aspiring teachers, and especially school administrators, for the conflict that occurs in schools. Conflict with students, parents, colleagues and supervisors is what wakes us up in the middle of the night with a pit in our stomach. Difficult conversations that have gone bad, are being avoided, or which will take place the next day grip our minds, dominate our self-talk, drain our emotional energy, and block us from being more present-centered. While there are technical bodies of knowledge that must be learned, far too little emphasis is placed on the emotional capacities that contribute to effective leadership.*

The knowledge and skills necessary for leaders to handle conflicts effectively are discussed in the next two lessons.

LESSON SIX

"The process of thinking requires feeling, for feelings are what let us understand all the information that we can't directly comprehend." Jonah Lehrer, How We Decide

In many years of working with aspiring administrators, I have discovered that learning to read and understand successfully one's own emotions, the emotions of others, and the information that emerges from this understanding is vital to learning how to manage conflict effectively. Emotions are packets of data. They contain important information that can amplify our knowledge about a problem or broaden our view of a situation. Learning to read emotions expands the data available to us. Becoming fluent in the world of emotions widens our bandwidth of knowledge.

Exercise emotional intelligence

EMOTIONAL AWARENESS

How strongly do you agree with the following statements?

1. It is unprofessional to bring emotions to the workplace.
2. Emotions distort the logical reasoning process that allows you to solve workplace problems.
3. If you show emotions at work, people will view you as weak.

In many ways, emotions are associated with being unprofessional. When educators are asked to respond to the statements above, they express widely diverse views. In general, they share a sense of worry, concern, and reticence about expressing or utilizing emotional information as part of their work. In their view, the domains of the professional include logic, reasoning detached from emotions, and quantitative data. Emotions are viewed as not helpful to the hard decision-making and analysis necessary for an effective educational leader. The professional who expresses emotions, with the exception of anger, is perceived as potentially lacking toughness and not fit for leadership.

The dilemma for leaders is that excluding emotions from one's work handicaps one's ability to successfully manage conflicts. Inevitably, one of the reasons that conflict is complex and uncomfortable is because of the embedded emotions that surround any problem. Handling conflicts well often relies first on recognizing the embedded emotions and then learning to manage them. By ignoring or denying the feelings within a situation, leaders are creating blind spots that prevent them from examining important data.

Jonah Lehrer, author of *How We Decide*, notes:

> *The emotional brain is especially useful at helping us make hard decisions. Its massive computational power — its ability to process millions of bits of data in parallel — ensures you can analyze all the relevant information when assessing alternatives. Mysteries are broken down into manageable chunks, which are then translated into practical feelings.*

The notion of bandwidth emerged one evening when I was helping my son study for a dreaded chemistry exam. As I perused the chapter the test covered, I noticed a diagram that illustrated the wavelengths of electromagnetic radiation. This depiction represented gamma rays with the shortest length and radio waves with the longest. In between these endpoints were names with which I had a little familiarity: X-rays, ultraviolet, infrared, and microwaves. This recognition, however, had nothing to do with my knowledge of electromagnetic waves. I just happened to encounter these terms in more practical arenas of my life. Unfortunately, my science background was built on too much memorization and too little understanding.

Despite my thin knowledge base in science, I found myself intrigued by a narrow band in the middle of this scientific illustration representing visible light. This strip represented a very small portion of the diagram. All the rest of the energy forms on the chart, by default, were invisible to the human eye. Proportionally, the ratio of visible to invisible reminded me of the broader spectrum of my life experiences. I have come to the conclusion that what I observe is only a very small part of what provides me with knowledge and wisdom. There is an entire domain of information that is constantly entering my field of experience outside my consciousness. With a lot of help from my wife, for example, I am now a little more aware of how my feelings can influence my behaviors. Learning to become emotionally fluent has been an invaluable tool in helping me be a better husband, father, and a more effective educational leader.

On most days, connecting my feelings to my actions is not a natural task. For a long time, I was not aware that I consistently had emotional reactions to situations, not to mention how those feelings might be influencing me. When my wife asked how I was feeling about a recent family visit, or how I was feeling about the evening we had spent at the neighbors, or how I was feeling about the telephone call I just had with my sister, I struggled to say more than "fine" or "O.K." Internally, I would wonder why my wife was even asking this question. It felt superfluous to the events and trivial.

I have come to appreciate, however, the utility in seeking out my underlying feelings and trying to understand what I am emotionally experiencing in a particular situation. I am beginning to understand better how embarrassment or insecurity in certain situations can lead me to become hostile or extremely quiet. By recognizing these feelings and their impact on my behavior, I have gained the ability to choose a different reaction under similar circumstances. As Al Mamary said, "knowledge is power!"

I have noticed a similar pattern with many students, whose moods often camouflage complex struggles that pull and tug against them in a variety of ways. There is little hope of being supportive to these students during their dark moments if we only stay on the surface and respond to their presenting behaviors. The grouchy bark of a teenager can easily lead away from conversation and into the domain of a heated verbal battle. Learning how not to react too strongly to the visible behavior of those who are angry or upset is a critical skill for educational leaders. Even more critical is learning how to see underneath the surface and understand the impact that the emotions of others have on you, the leader.

Daniel Goleman's research has revealed important skills that emerge as we develop our emotional intelligence. Emotional intelligence, as Goleman has defined it, "does not mean giving free reign to feelings" or "letting it all hang out." Rather, it means "managing feelings so that they are expressed appropriately and effectively, enabling people to work together smoothly toward their common goals." Self-awareness, conscientiousness, motivation, empathy, and collaboration are a small sample of the skills we can gain from enhancing our emotional prowess. Most of us are still in our infancy in learning how to explicitly develop these skills. One way for educators to support this learning is to find the time and the means to unpack the events of their days. Heifetz describes the importance of "getting on the balcony" or disengaging from the current swirl of activity on the dance floor in order to "observe and gain perspective on yourself and on the larger system." This process enables one to "see patterns that are not visible from the ground." Our daily encounters can affect us in unforeseen but comprehensible ways. Appreciating and understanding the patterns of our emotions can help us better analyze our errors, understand the choices we make, and expand the options we have available to us.

Jerome Groopman, in his book, *How Doctors Think*, makes this point in relation to doctors:

> *But what I and my colleagues rarely recognized, and what physicians still rarely discussed as medical students...is how other emotions influence a doctor's perceptions and judgments, his actions and reactions. I long believed that the errors we made in medicine were largely technical ones – prescribing the wrong dose of a drug, transfusing a unit of blood matched for another person, mislabeling an x-ray of an arm as 'right' instead of 'left.' But as a growing body of research shows, technical errors account for only a small fraction of our incorrect diagnoses and treatments. Most errors are mistakes in thinking. And a part of what causes these cognitive errors is our inner feelings, feelings we do not readily admit to and often don't even recognize.*

Being adept at reading emotions is not the same as being emotional and does not imply any actions. Awareness of one's own or another's emotion does not demand a particular emotional response. For example, detecting sadness in oneself or others does not mean one has to cry at work.

Another common misconception about emotions in the workplace is that they are only present when there is a major conflict or an intense problem or experience. While stress, tension, and difficulties will generate strong emotions, feelings are present all the time. The challenge is not in recognizing emotional information during charged circumstances but in accurately reading the emotional landscape on a regular basis.

Deborah Tannen's book, *I Only Say This Because I Love You*, uses several examples to illustrate how omnipresent and embedded emotions are in every day events.

> A dinnertime conversation:
> *Irene and David are looking over their menus in a restaurant. David says he will order a steak. Irene says, "Did you notice they also have salmon?"*

This vignette does not describe a complex issue or a tension riddled event and yet it is potentially packed with emotions. What was Irene feeling when she made her comment? What is our best guess of what David was feeling after he heard Irene's comment?

When I present this scene to administrators, some hypothesize that David might feel angry or bothered by Irene's possible interference with his choice. Others think that Irene is motivated by concern for David or simply trying to encourage an alternative choice. While we don't know for sure what either person was feeling, those who consider this situation "from the balcony" have no problem seeing a wide range of potential feelings.

> An email sent from a principal to his staff:
> *It is that time of year again. I need to observe one of your classes. Please invite me in to see your best teaching. Arrange a mutually convenient time with my secretary for this observation.*

The principal's intention was to capture in his observations some lessons that would amplify the staff's strengths. He was surprised to discover that there was a strong emotional reaction to the email. Some teachers were concerned that the principal wanted them to put on a "dog and pony show." Others were upset that the first line sounded like supervision was a mundane task, rather than an important aspect of the educational process for the principal. Some teachers were concerned that they had to make an appointment through a secretary.

Both the Irene and David vignette and the principal's email are typical of the innocuous day-to-day exchanges that occur in and around the schoolhouse. It is possible to ignore the underlying emotions contained within these situations. However, it is not unusual that the ignored emotions will seep out in other situations and, when they do, become more complex and difficult to manage.

The skills related to reading and managing emotions are tangential to the work of leadership and central to the responsibility of developing professional relationships. Doug Reeves includes the following emotional competencies in his listing of essential leadership dimensions:

1. Emotional self-control reflecting an appropriate response to situations
2. Constructive reaction to disappointment; willingness to admit error and learn from failure
3. Constructive handling of disagreement and dissent

ACKNOWLEDGEMENT

One of the most critical skills related to emotional fluency is acknowledgment. Acknowledgment is the act of recognizing, appreciating, and valuing the emotions present in another. To utilize acknowledgement effectively, the resulting communication must be wholehearted and genuine. Individuals cannot bargain their acknowledgement by putting on conditions such as expecting the other individual to appreciate your perspective.

Effective acknowledgment is not the same as agreement. It may also include taking responsibility for the impact of the emotional situation. It is fully possible to acknowledge a belief or feeling and still hold a different perspective. For many people, acknowledgment of another's perspective is equated with acknowledging wrongdoing. For example, being willing to listen to another point of view is equated with losing. Acknowledging the feelings present in others, however, is often a necessary first step to constructing mutual understanding of a situation, problem, or event.

LESSON SIX

There are two specific sub skills related to effective acknowledgment: 1) spotting the feelings present in others and 2) communicating an understanding of those feelings. The second skill is more complex and challenging because, for many leaders, the understanding is equated with agreeing with the other party completely.

In order to effectively acknowledge, one must be in tune with the emotions that are present in a conversation - both the feelings of the other person and your own. This awareness must then be successfully applied in a way that manages the emotions. It must positively direct what one does and says.

The following examples demonstrated for me the impact of acknowledgement. A series of email exchanges between a parent and me occurred when I was a principal. The parent was upset when she found out that a math teacher I had hired was let go. Her anger was focused on the fact that, when she found out that the teacher was let go, she realized that her son's complaints about this teacher were valid. She realized that the deficits she had attributed to her son as a student were in fact due to poor instruction from the teacher.

> First email from the parent:
>
> *Dr. D'Auria,*
>
> *I am so disappointed in your administration for hiring Mr. Dode last year. I am a doctor at Beth Israel Hospital and today I heard from a patient that Mr. Dode was let go or whatever due to inability. I so resent the impact he had on my son, Roger, who now doesn't like math. You kept this teacher on for what reason? We struggled through last year with a lot of angst and not a lot of Mr. Dode helping by sending us data about our son. I blame the administration for letting this marginal math experience happen. How do you explain this? I need an explanation from your office as your administration has really ruined my son's attitude about math, which is an important language in our world.*
>
> *Dr. Leonard*

My first reply:

Dear Dr. Leonard,

I am sorry about the experience your son Roger had with Mr. Dode. I would be happy to discuss the situation with you as well as how Roger is doing this year with his new teacher. When is a good time to call you and what number should I use to contact you?

John

Second email from the parent:

Dr. D'Auria,

I don't need to talk about Mr Dode — but I think that the students should have been told that they were not 100% responsible for the year of math they experienced. I was always impressed at your observation that young people in middle school could solve any problem many different ways... And I think that the experience they had, at least in our case, was really discouraging. For me, the validation from the school would have been a useful repair. I am not in this equation so I am not going to inform Roger of this. I guess he will have to realize that he is not always wrong. The teacher this year is fine so far, but it is not his job to repair last year's effects. Thanks for the time. Roger does not know I am writing you. He would probably be mortified.

Harriet Leonard

My second reply:

Dear Harriet,

I, too, am very disappointed in the results of some of my decisions. I wish that I could say that all my hires have been terrifically successful ones. Unfortunately, that is not the case. Your point about acknowledging to the students that the adults contributed to their struggles is an important one. You have given me food for thought. I would be very happy to talk to Roger. I perhaps could interview him and a few other students from Mr. Dode's classes and, thereby, as part of this after the fact analysis, insert my perspective.

John

Final email from the parent:

Thank you for offering to talk to Roger. I could not predict if he would ever be candid about last year's experience. I realize that not all teachers are A plus - and I appreciate your statements. I think the people you are leading are in a difficult position. Thanks. I am not trying to be a "helicopter parent" and he is working hard – so that's all we really want. This year he seems pretty happy. Thanks.

Harriet

In the progression of this exchange, there is a detectable shift that occurs in the parent's tone, which was preceded by several acknowledgements that I made. The change took place, I believe, as a result of my willingness to acknowledge not only the parent's feelings and concerns but also my own responsibility in the matter. This combination of conveying an understanding of what others are feeling and a willingness to take responsibility for the impact that has occurred is an important fulcrum that can create movement in what starts out as a no-win situation.

A second email was forwarded by a parent to a principal. The parent had received this email about her daughter from the daughter's teacher.

Hi Mr. And Mrs. Blake,

I am still seeing the silly, argumentative behaviors in Shaakira. She came late without a pass on Wednesday and did not attend her required extra help session. I am feeling as though these weekly reports are not helping the situation and frankly feel frustrated that I never have any response from you. I'd like to entertain the idea of ceasing these weekly reports. I have no other plan at this point to put in its place. I am open to any suggestions you might have.

The principal who received this email from the parent shared with me that he was first ashamed and then angry with the teacher for writing what he viewed as an insensitive email. However, before acting on these emotions, the principal decided to ask the teacher what she was feeling when she wrote the email. To the principal's surprise, the teacher expressed "loneliness." The principal was expecting to hear words like "angry" or "frustrated." Instead, the teacher shared that she felt incredibly isolated as she dealt with this very challenging case. Once the principal heard this feeling expressed, he was able to acknowledge it and take some responsibility for not sufficiently supporting the teacher with this very complex student case. The principal also mentioned that he did not refrain from sharing with the teacher that her expression of her feelings in the email was neither effective nor in keeping with the standards of the school. This critique, however, was made after acknowledging her feelings. It was the acknowledgement that helped to make the conversation more productive.

Neither of these examples gives a full picture of the complexity and challenge that educational leaders face on a daily basis. However, the vignettes contain a rich assortment of emotions that left unattended can easily morph into concerns that will have significant impact on morale, culture, and the quality of the professional relationships that exist within a school community. As skillful teachers know, it is by paying attention to the little details that the bigger problems are prevented in a classroom. Similarly, leaders who pay immediate attention to the less complex but important issues will have fewer significant issues emerge in their school communities.

LESSON SEVEN

"The gap between what you're really thinking and what you're saying is part of what makes a conversation difficult." Stone, Patton, Heen, & Fisher

Schools abound with potential conflict. There are philosophical differences among and between teachers and administrators. There are disagreements around approaches to teaching and learning between parents and teachers. Grading, discipline, and limited resources all produce possibilities for strong emotions and significant disagreements. It is part of the responsibility of leaders to manage these disagreements and tensions so that they neither lay dormant and erode morale nor erupt explosively and produce damaged relationships that impede teaching or learning. Within the seeds of disagreement and conflict are also ideas and perspectives that can potentially help to create better programs, interventions, and responses to the problems that a particular teacher, administrator, or school community faces. One must view conflict as a potential ally.

Exercise emotional intelligence

In order to transform one's perspective about conflict from a negative interaction to a positive framework, a leader must master and apply a number of skills related to transforming conflicts into learning. As we have discussed above, open and honest communication as well as emotional fluency are essential to conflict resolution. Another important set of skills relate to managing the difficult conversations that make us anxious and that we want to avoid.

In developing my own skills in managing these conversations, I have benefitted from the research that Douglas Stone, Bruce Patton, and Sheila Heen present in their book, *Difficult Conversations: How to Discuss What Matters Most*. Drawing on their research, three skills and concepts emerge that that are necessary and important for leaders to master if they are to be successful with difficult conversations:

1. Be curious in response to what feels like criticism and a verbal attack.
2. Recognize that good intentions do not sanitize bad impact.
3. Abandon blame and map the contribution system.

1. BE CURIOUS IN RESPONSE TO WHAT FEELS LIKE CRITICISM AND A VERBAL ATTACK.

It is very difficult to give up our certainties – our positions, our beliefs, our explanations... Yet I believe we will succeed in changing this world only if we can think and work together in new ways. Curiosity is what we need. We don't have to let go of what we believe but we do need to be curious about what someone else believes.

Margaret Wheatley

The overarching principle to master in order to navigate successfully the choppy waters of difficult conversations is to understand that these conversations are not about the truth, but about conflicting perceptions, values, and interpretations. While schools are essentially about teaching and learning, communication is often the nexus of our operations. It is not unusual for school improvement plans to call for improved communication among and between constituencies. Despite volumes of newsletters, phone calls, emails, and face-to-face meetings, building a common understanding between parents and educators, teachers and administrators, staff and colleagues, is an ongoing challenge. Communication between these groups can, at times be uncomfortable, delicate, and emotionally charged. Avoiding the potentially painful aspects of such a discourse can make the original problem or concern more complicated.

When school issues emerged involving one of my own children, despite my experience in education, I had to fight off the urge to avoid or postpone calling the teacher. If I neglected to act promptly, the issue did not go away and sometimes got worse. In these instances, in place of having a conversation, I engaged in a diatribe. Instead of being curious, I became combative. I did less listening and more talking.

Arguments can be won and lost that way, but rarely is mutual understanding a byproduct of such behavior. When a concern is raised about our child, it is not unusual for our eyes and ears to start selecting additional data that reinforce our

LESSON SEVEN

perspective. While our senses are not lying to us, our reinforced perspective can be a result of the "Ladder of Inference." The concept of a "Ladder of Inference" was developed by Peter Senge and his associates at MIT. It describes a sequence of events that often provide a fertile breeding ground for misunderstanding. The first rung of the ladder begins with a simple observation or experience. The next rung involves selecting certain information from the multitude of data points available from this experience. This step is key because what we select, by default, is not the whole picture – we discard some of the data. Our cultural and personal histories come into play as we add meaning to our data set. Based on the meaning we derive, we then develop assumptions. The assumptions lead us to conclusions that help us to form our beliefs about the world and direct us to an action. Our beliefs then influence future communication.

The ladder shows how we short circuit gaining important information. We may filter out data because we miss some points or block or illuminate certain details, while enhancing or diminishing others because of our basic belief structure. Each rung of the ladder demonstrates how information is missed or distorted by the limitations of our ability to listen as well as by our preconceptions, biases, and values. The sequence of steps illustrated by the Ladder of Inference should be expected in a world that contains vast amounts of data and information. The ladder describes a process that is fraught with opportunities to create significant misunderstanding, inaccurate portraits of people or situations, and ineffective communication.

Source: The Fifth Discipline Fieldbook, Senge et al, 1994.

A personal example of this communication sequence started when I was watching a basketball game in which my son was a player. It was one of those games that seemed magical. His shots were falling; passes were hitting their mark; he was also able to dribble his way through a few tight spots. At the end of the game, I was talking with another dad, who commented, "Boy, your son is such a ball hog." While I noted this derogatory comment, I put on my best "game face" because I did not have the courage to share any of my genuine feelings at the time. As I told my wife about the conversation, both of us became increasingly upset with the comments from this dad, whom we considered a "nice guy." By the next day, this "nice guy" had increasingly become the target of our criticisms and negative judgments. I dared not discuss this issue with him initially, thinking that by bringing it up directly I would be making too much of it. Little did I realize at the time how monumental the whole incident was becoming. My wife and I began to "notice" more insensitive behaviors by this person. All of this "data" was creating a significant wedge between us and this fellow parent and neighbor. Finally, on another day when I was at yet another gym watching another game, much to my chagrin I found myself sitting next to him. Deciding to take the plunge, I mustered some courage and said, "You know, when you called my son a ball hog, it stung. I wasn't sure how you came to that conclusion." He turned to me and said, "Ball hog? I said, Ball hawk." He followed up by explaining that his expression was meant as a compliment.

Oops! A lot of wasted energy, negative feelings, and distorted "fact-finding" resulted from a misheard word and from all the meanings, assumptions, and conclusions I had drawn from this "data." To this day, I am very grateful that I took the time to share my feelings that afternoon and demonstrate curiosity when I mentioned, "I wasn't sure how you came to that conclusion."

Over my career, I have experienced the effects of the Ladder of Inference as they play out in the variances in the data that parents and teachers "see." While children's stories can represent an accurate portrayal of events, there are other times when parents, students, and educators get stuck on one of the rungs of the Ladder. Someone hears or sees a piece of data and, from that partial set of information, assumptions and meanings are attached. This discrepancy is compounded because it is not always easy for parents to pick up the phone and check out with the teacher something they have heard from their children. As a result, they are likely to sit on the problem without gathering "other" perspectives in the early stages of an emerging issue. If their child continues to complain, sometimes they begin to collect their own "data." This new information gets added to their assumptions and before they know it, they are angry and upset before they even have had a chance to check out their notions directly with the teacher. Sides are drawn, feelings harden, and defensiveness replaces openness. Each of these communication snafus is akin to plaque that builds up in an artery and contributes to eroding morale and confidence in the school.

An important antidote and the central tenet of difficult conversations is curiosity. The act of being curious and asking questions in order to gain important information is a critical way to move off of the Ladder of Inference. We rarely show curiosity about each other's perspectives. Rather, we argue or defend our version of the truth without realizing that there is important information to which we don't have access. Being able to move from certainty to curiosity is a basic skill for holding difficult conversations.

2. RECOGNIZE THAT GOOD INTENTIONS DO NOT SANITIZE BAD IMPACT.

Rarely have I confronted a problem that had its roots in someone's bad intentions. Teachers' interventions with students are based on the belief that their actions will help students. Administrators' actions may cause anger or distress among teachers and parents, but rarely if ever are they intended to achieve that outcome. Yet, despite these good intentions, parents get upset with teachers, teachers get upset with administrators, administrators get upset with parents and teachers. However, after facilitating hundreds of meetings in which participants were upset with one another, I have rarely found that one party's announcement that he or she had the "best of intentions" produced a productive resolution of the problem. In fact, the announcement of one's good intentions can have the opposite effect: people get more upset.

The challenge in managing difficult conversations is that, for many people, acknowledging impact feels like losing or admitting fault. Acknowledging impact is tantamount to recognizing that an individual's actions had an effect that was not intended on another person. Acknowledging and appreciating these feelings increases the likelihood that genuine listening and understanding can occur.

A school with a mostly white faculty had two African American staff members, one of whom was the Director of the METCO Program (a voluntary desegregation program) and the other was a counselor in the METCO Program. The Director came to the principal of the school because a number of white staff members were consistently calling her by the name of the other African American staff member. While the METCO Director could understand how this might happen occasionally, she felt it was happening too frequently to be ignored. She asked the principal if she could share her observations at a faculty meeting and the principal encouraged her. As she told her story, the initial reaction of some staff was to suggest that being called by the wrong name had happened to them at some point at this large school. The Director became more, not less, upset with their observations. As she became angrier, other staff offered additional explanations that communicated the good intentions of the staff. None of the comments made the METCO Director feel better. The principal intervened when he saw that this exchange was making matters worse and asked for the staff to come back to the discussion the next day. At the second meeting, one staff member began by saying she had thought about what the Director had shared. She acknowledged that "as one of only two African Americans in the school, you must feel isolated here. To be called by the wrong name must reinforce your feelings that we are not a very welcoming staff. I am sorry that this has been your experience." This teacher did not seek to excuse the hurt of the Director with good intentions. Rather, she acknowledged the impact of being addressed by the wrong name. This approach facilitated a fruitful dialogue about how the staff could spend more time getting to know one another better.

The Director of Performing Arts and the Principal of a school received the following email:

The annual winter concert has just finished. As a Jewish member of this school community, I want to share my discomfort over some parts of this assembly with you.

LESSON SEVEN

For many American Jews, December is the month of the year during which we are most reminded of our "minority" status in the U.S. Many of our most symbolic public spaces – everything from the White House to Wal-Mart to television – send the message that to be truly a part of America, one must celebrate the birth of Christ.

I am usually very proud of the way that our staff and students embrace the diversity of cultures, races, religions, and sexual preferences at our school. However, I felt that today's concert was often a Christmas/Christian assembly masquerading as a secular winter celebration. The specific parts that were uncomfortable for me were the lighted Christmas tree at the entrance of the auditorium, the first song asking God to bless America, and a song that repeated, "Merry Christmas, Merry Christmas." I am confident that the staff who chose to include these elements in the concert did not intend to make anyone feel excluded, but that was exactly how I felt. It was a very painful shock to attend an event that I'd been looking forward to with anticipation, only to be met with so many symbols that seemed to be saying: "This is not your assembly. You don't belong here. Our school culture does not include you."

I know our school has the potential to make every school member feel included as an equal citizen. Today, however, I felt that we did not meet this standard. I am particularly sensitive to these issues, and there might not be a single other person who left the assembly feeling as I did. Nonetheless, I wouldn't feel right leaving the building today without sharing these feelings with you.

Even if all the parties in these situations were to express their good intentions to each other, deeper understanding would not be the result. The conversations would not move forward. The principal in the first scenario faces a tough challenge because he needs each party to acknowledge the impact the events had on the other. For the teacher in the second scenario, the experience of feeling like the other as a result of what she observed had a negative impact. For the Performing Arts Director, who had devoted weeks of preparation to producing a beautiful concert that respected the diversity of the community, the impact was that she did not feel appreciated for these efforts. It is also relevant that she did not appreciate having the email cc'd to her boss.

3. ABANDON BLAME AND MAP THE CONTRIBUTION SYSTEM.

Don't fix the blame, fix the problem. Japanese saying

If one hovered a thousand feet over a school community and had the ability to listen in on multiple conversations over time, one would hear a substantial amount of blame. Administrators blame the union; teachers blame administrators; parents blame teachers; educators blame municipal government; citizens blame the teachers' contract; and on it goes.

The expression of blame is often grounded in substantive problems –but the act of blaming rarely produces effective solutions. Talking about fault is similar to talking about truth because it produces disagreement, denial, and minimal learning. It evokes fears of punishment and insists on an either-or-answer. Fear is toxic to learning. Without a concerted effort to limit the effects of fear, learning opportunities for students will be limited.

No one wants to be blamed, especially unfairly, so our energy goes into defending ourselves. Fear and defensiveness block learning. Instead of understanding our errors, we become angry and closed to learning from our mistakes. It is particularly damaging in a school environment to have fear and anger choke off learning because learning is our main activity.

My experience as an educator has helped me to understand that there are four big fears that are often present for our students:

- Fear of making mistakes
- Fear of looking like a fool
- Fear of having a weakness exposed
- Fear of failure

Teachers also experience fear. The big four fears for teachers are:
- Fear of making mistakes
- Fear that errors will erase prior success
- Fear of having a weakness exposed
- Fear that asking for assistance will diminish respect and make the teacher look like a novice

Part of the responsibility of effective educational leadership involves diminishing the inhibitive effects of fear on learning. Schools that are effective limit the effects of fear and create a safe environment for learning. One way to create this safe environment is to abandon blame.

Effective leaders distinguish blame from contribution. Blame is about judging and looking backward. It hinders problem solving and often targets an individual or a singular party. When blame is the goal, understanding is the casualty. Contribution is about understanding and looking forward. Focusing on contributions encourages learning and change. Contribution looks to the subtle elements that may contribute to a problem.

A custodial union issue illustrates the effectiveness of substituting "mapping the contribution system" for "assessing blame." Custodial issues were one of the most contentious areas in the district to which I newly arrived as superintendent. Financial conditions within the district, combined with a long standing concern for the quality of service that was delivered, influenced the School Committee to investigate rigorously the outsourcing of our cleaning services. This action led the Union to break off negotiations and demand impact bargaining with a negotiator. Prior to the start of the bargaining session, I had a chance to interview principals, inspect buildings, and hear the concerns of central office staff and the School Committee. During one of my early visits to a school building, the principal pulled me aside and informed me that one of the custodians wanted to have a "private word" with me. The custodian shared how proud he was of his work and the building that he cleaned. He also told me how upset he was that the administration, by its actions, had "condemned" the entire unit because of the poor work of a few individuals. I listened and summarized what I heard in his message, including not only his main points but the feelings that went along with them. The custodian thanked me for taking the time to talk with him and let me know that in the nearly three decades of his work in our schools, this was the first time he had ever spoken with a superintendent.

I took my learnings from this interchange to the negotiation table. I started the bargaining session by summarizing what I had gleaned from my rounds through each of the schools. My summary did not include blame. It explained the concerns of administrators and School Committee members and their desire for consistent quality. I indicated that I thought that these issues were translated in a way that did not distinguish workers who were doing a terrific job. This acknowledgement went a long way toward "breaking the logjam" and opening a dialogue. I also shared that while there were significant concerns about the performance quality of certain individuals, there was no paper trail of unsatisfactory evaluations because administrators had not performed evaluations. The previous contract was vague about the evaluation process. This vagueness led administrators to believe that their documentation would not hold up if a case went to arbitration. As a result of this finding, I suggested that administrators had to take ownership of some of the problems that we were experiencing as a district. It was this acknowledgement of people, the evaluation process, and other factors that were contributing to the problem that helped to move the negotiation process forward. At the end of negotiations - in a very tough financial period, we settled on a 0% Cost of Living, a new and reduced salary schedule for new employees, and a revised and clearer evaluation system. With these concessions, the School Committee dropped its interest in outsourcing. We had an opportunity to start anew with a one-year contract and to gain positive momentum prior to the start of another round of contract negotiations.

Acting according to the principle of "Abandon Blame and Map the Contribution System" is not an easy task. It starts with understanding the dynamics of blame. Blame can be understood as a weather vane that signals the existence of strong, unexpressed feelings lurking underground. Expressing these feelings more directly and accurately can go a long way toward building understanding about what went wrong. When I blame my wife or my children for some mistake, it often masks my worry, embarrassment, or concern. Had I the courage to say, "I am worried" or "I am embarrassed," rather than "Why the heck did you…?," defensiveness might be replaced more frequently with ownership.

Capturing the camouflaged emotions underneath the act of blaming is one part of the theory of mapping the contribution system. The other aspect of this framework is that no problem, no disappointment, and no break down is solely one party's fault. There usually is a system of small and large actions, made by the stakeholders, that collectively contribute to the problem at hand. By examining contributions, individuals and organizational teams can learn from their mistakes and reduce the probability that a similar error will be made in the future. The truly difficult challenge, however, is to understand one's own contribution, especially when we feel that the egregious fault lies elsewhere.

When we find ourselves wondering what we could possibly have contributed to a problem that seems so obviously someone else's fault, we should consider silence as one of the common but often missed contributions. Sometimes we do not express our disagreement or concern because we did not want to put a burden on another person. Other times we wait for a related, larger, more substantive issue to arise. By remaining silent, we often create a larger, more complex issue. What starts out as an easy problem often becomes increasingly complicated by silence and unexpressed concerns. This dynamic is vividly captured in a poem attributed to Pastor Martin Niemoller as he described the impact of silence in the face of Nazis actions:

> *When the Nazis came for the communists,*
> *I remained silent; I was not a communist.*
> *When they locked up the social democrats,*
> *I remained silent; I was not a social democrat.*
> *When they came for the trade unionists,*
> *I did not speak out; I was not a trade unionist.*
> *When they came for me, there was no one left to speak out.*

There are so many reasons to pass up an opportunity to comment critically. We are too busy. We don't want to rock the boat. We don't want to hurt someone's feelings. We don't want to damage a vital relationship. If leaders are doing their jobs, they create environments that value crucial commentary, heated debate, and constructive feedback. Valuing these expressions does not relieve individuals, however, of the responsibility of speaking out, speaking up, and sharing their concerns early and often.

It has taken a long time to learn the lesson of not keeping silent, and it is one I easily forget. Receiving a critical email, a harsh voice mail, or a complaint after a long and arduous day can often feel like an insensitive blow to the solar plexus. However, somewhere in the criticism left on my desk, I need to find the pearl that cannot be dismissed. Unearthing that valuable piece of information is the essence of effective communication and it is what helps organizations to grow. The individuals who take the time to reveal their concerns before these issues become a larger problem make a contribution, despite the discomfort that they may create.

The dynamics of silence also play out in our classrooms. When students receive a poor grade or experience a disappointing outcome, they also must choose between attributing blame and mapping the contribution system. Some students will blame themselves: "I am stupid; I am not a math person." Others will blame the teacher: "He's mean." "She is not helpful."

While teachers have an important role to play in how well students learn, students also contribute to their own achievement. Our more successful students look to themselves when they experience failure or disappointment. They consider how they have contributed to the problem and make the necessary adjustments. Similarly, master teachers look to themselves when their students fail in order to improve their outreach or their pedagogy.

While the phrase "Abandon Blame and Map the Contribution System" is easy to say, it is difficult to follow. When you spot the trappings of blame, seek to understand the underlying feelings and examine the strategies and behaviors that might have led to a disappointing outcome. This technique will improve our teaching, our collegial relationships, our parenting, and most importantly, our learning.

Lesson EIGHT

"This meeting was like many of the meetings that I would go to over the course of two years. The only way I can describe it is that, well, the president is like a blind man in a roomful of deaf people. There is no discernible connection." Paul O'Neil

"The problem is most managers don't know how to hold an effective meeting, much less bring up sensitive issues in a way that fosters team building and open communication." Marlene Chism

Use meetings (of all types) to increase academic focus

Each year when I present leadership ideas to a new cohort of aspiring administrators, I ask them to share their perspective about the general value of the meetings they attend throughout the year. Unfortunately, most report that meetings rank somewhere between worthless and benign. A high percentage of my students report that their experience in meetings is the antithesis of learning. For many, meetings are akin to watching paint dry.

Assuming that these informal assessments are accurate, a number of serious issues are raised. If one were to calculate the cost of these meetings, one could imagine that there were better ways to spend the thousands of dollars that are being expended on the salaries of those in attendance. Meetings provide subtle but powerful signals about expectations about teaching, learning, and the importance of questioning, debate, and wrestling with complex ideas. If meetings are passive experiences in which information is dispensed but ideas are not discussed, it is possible that teachers may internalize this model and make connections with the expectations for their classroom teaching. It is not a stretch to think that teachers may wonder if this "sit and git" approach is how their teaching should be delivered.

Like biological systems, school systems have a complex set of interactions and dynamics that are influenced by a code that ties the entire system into an interactive unit. The code in the case of schools is not related to genetics but to the patterns of teaching and learning established over time by both the leaders and the staff. Every time a teaching opportunity presents itself, it is both reflective of the dynamics of the system and an influence on how the system will operate in the future.

Once this dynamic became clear to me as a principal, I began to realize that meetings serve a dual purpose. They not only help to advance an agenda -either stated or unstated, but they convey the expectations, beliefs, and models of teaching and learning embraced by the leader. It follows logically that meetings should look very similar to effective classroom lessons. They should convey important ideas, skills, and concepts. They should pay attention to pedagogical parameters such as objectives, activities, and momentum, all of which are critical to active engagement. Meetings should model for the staff the leader's values regarding teaching and learning. When there is a dissonance between what is said at meetings and how teaching is expected to be delivered, the verbal message can easily be overshadowed by that which is being modeled.

- Any school faces a series of questions that are challenging to answer:
- How can we keep standards high and increase student engagement?
- How do we support our special education students without lowering expectations?
- What rules should we all agree to uphold and what discretion do we want to give to individual teachers?
- How can we increase the number of students who qualify for honors courses?
- How consistent should our grading processes be?
- To what degree should homework factor into a final grade?
- Should students be able to retake exams after a poor performance?

- How frequently and for what reasons should parents be contacted?
- How much should test scores weigh in determining final grades?
- What are the advantages and disadvantages of specializing instruction (departmentalization) in upper elementary grades?
- Does grouping students by skill level lead to better achievement for all groups?

These questions represent only a small percentage of the challenging topics that school faculties could study, discuss, argue about, and resolve for their school community. Department leaders, directors, principals, and central office administrators can develop common standards for pedagogy by grappling with the many issues and differences of opinion that arise. Creating productive meetings that allow for discussion and disagreement requires the same pedagogical skills that teachers apply in their classroom lessons.

A good meeting agenda is only part of the challenge, however. Creating an atmosphere in which staff feel comfortable enough to honestly share their views, report on their failures as well as their successes, and disagree with colleagues is more challenging than designing a skillfully crafted meeting agenda. The odds of creating engaging agendas improves immensely when there is collaboration. The leader does not have to plan meetings alone and every meeting does not have to be an exemplar. The effective leader constantly tinkers with how to turn meetings into learning experiences that maximize the impact of the time invested. The leader also is always open to feedback from the meeting participants and is modeling for teachers what they can do with feedback from their students through formative assessments, student work, and performance data.

Jennifer Henderson, an elementary school principal, applies the "lesson design" concept to meetings when she wants the staff to contribute its thinking on topics impacting the school. She calls this strategy "Think Abouts." Jennifer utilizes easel sheets that are posted around the room and headed with reflection topics. The teachers are randomly assigned to small groups who each station themselves at one of the easel sheets. Using packs of "sticky notes," the teachers reflect on the "think about" topic, write their ideas on the sticky notes, and post the notes on the easel paper. The group of teachers then move on to the next easel sheet and repeat the process until they have added notes to each of the easel sheets. Sometimes Jennifer heads the easel paper with a question that can be answered with a yes/no/maybe answer, but typically "think about" topics require several phrases. Topics for "think abouts" have included a concern that she seeks feedback on, an issue or idea that a staff member or parent has raised, and ideas for instructional strategies. Think abouts are also used to gauge how the school's values are being reflected in the school's culture. At the end of the "Think About," the comments on the sticky notes are summarized so that at a future staff meeting they can be shared, discussed, and analyzed.

Sample think abouts:

- An idea from a recent workshop that is worth exploring further
- A strategy that has helped students who struggle with organization
- Effective ways of involving families new to your classroom
- Books that help students move from being a bystander to an "upstander"

LESSON EIGHT

A department head wanted to utilize a research article to jumpstart a conversation about alternative grading practices. She worried about having a conversation that would be dominated by a few individuals and was concerned that some would attend the meeting not having read the article. Her decision to provide time in the meeting for reading the article was greatly appreciated by staff. She asked participants, as they read, to underline a part of the article that grabbed their attention. When it was time to discuss the article, she used Jon Saphier's strategy, the "Last Word," to launch the discussion. In this approach, one person shares a quote from the article but does not explain why this text was selected. The person next to the participant who offered the quote gives his or her reaction to the text, followed by the others in the group. After all of the participants present their perspective, the original person has the "Final Word" and explains why he or she found the quote important, intriguing, or upsetting. The group concludes this discussion with a mini debriefing and a second person begins the same process with a new quote from the text. This technique ensures that no one person dominates the conversation and gives people who normally are quiet an opportunity to participate actively. Following this discussion, the department head initiated a discussion on aspects of their own grading systems that faculty members might want to experiment with, based on the ideas presented in the article.

The same principles that apply to faculty meetings apply to encounters among and between professionals. In *The Six Secrets of Change*, Michael Fullan uses the phrase "Learning is the Work" to explain his belief that it is the learning that takes place in the classroom that creates more skilled teaching and more expert teachers. Fullan notes that in the typical school, professional development is defined as workshops or courses that are taken off site and taught by professionals outside of the system. Faculty meetings, department meetings, and "teacher talk" in the hallway are viewed as outside the realm of professional development. However, he stresses, these interactions can and should be the richest form of learning for educators. Any opportunity that brings together professionals to discuss problems with the aim of finding solutions or improving student learning is a form of professional development. Fullen writes that "Deep learning ... is embedded in the culture of the workplace." Skillful leaders understand the value of mining every opportunity for developing and sharing insights into the complex issues their learning communities face.

Lesson NINE

Regardless of our contexts, our circumstances, or the needs of our schools, educational leaders are constantly facing three important choices:

Greatness vs. Maintenance
Courage vs. Caution
Autonomy vs. Dependency

GREATNESS VS. MAINTENANCE

Greatness might be a word that seems over the top in describing the choices that principals, superintendents, or other educational leaders face daily, but I think it is quite apt. Maintaining the day-to-day operation of schools threatens to consume school leaders. Every leader has a long list of responsibilities such as keeping the buses running on time, insuring that the lunch room is clean before the students leave, sending report cards out on time, answering emails promptly, helping parents with a fundraiser, counting and packing up state tests, preparing for a flu clinic, writing a newsletter, handling discipline, hiring a new teacher, and attending a team meeting. The list is never finished because as one job is completed, ten more are added. If one is not vigilant, maintenance becomes a full time job.

Furthermore, the regular tasks can sometimes obscure opportunities to take the school community in new and exciting directions. Resisting the temptation to focus only on maintenance priorities can result in unexpected benefits. Examining grade patterns at a middle school might lead to investigating the benefits of altering or eliminating a tracking system. Analyzing data from parent interviews, when backed up by research studies, might lead a high school principal to consider a different approach for including special education students in mainstream classes. An elementary school principal who is trying to improve math achievement might consider platooning staff so that during the math block students can be subdivided into small groups in order to receive targeted instruction. Each of these possibilities could pose an enormous risk to the status quo and stability of the school. Any of these possibilities might

Remember the choices that constantly present themselves

75

unleash a strong and angry reaction from parents, faculty, or students. It is this sense of unease, and the balance of significant risk vs. significant gain, that leads to the realization that a choice is emerging. It is at this juncture that a leader chooses between greatness and maintenance.

COURAGE VS. CAUTION

There comes a critical juncture for most leaders when new knowledge, new research, and new information are not enough. Taking a school or district from where it is to where the leader wants it to go will require the courage to not have to know every possible permutation and combination that one might encounter after the leap. Courage becomes a factor as one engages in due diligence and assesses the risk factors. Courage is an absolute requirement of effective leadership.

> *Doug Dias, a high school principal in a predominantly white district that has seen a rapid influx of African American students, alerted his staff to an incident in the school's cafeteria with the following message:*
>
> *I am sending this email to inform you of an event that occurred in the cafeteria during third lunch on Wednesday. Several black girls became extremely upset over a prejudiced and racist text message that had been sent by a white student to another white student the prior evening. The recipient shared the inflammatory content of the message with two friends who, in turn, shared their outrage with several of their black friends, who were offended and upset. They went to the table in the cafeteria where the student who had sent the text was seated and confronted him, expressing their outrage. Students at the table were unaware of the context, and tried to make light of the situation, not knowing all of the details of the incident, which further upset the girls.*
>
> *As the teachers in the cafeteria dealt with the situation, and sent one student out of the cafeteria, a separate table of senior boys, unaware of the specifics on the incident, began pounding on the table and chanting. The two instigators of this action were sent to the office.*
>
> *I spoke with several of the students directly involved and believe that this incident uncovers a problem.*

LESSON NINE

Racism exists all around us in our society and in every town and high school in America. Our school is no exception. While some may rationalize the event as a series of bad decisions, I believe that there is more to it. Racist language is simply an unacceptable form of self-expression; it violates my core values and the core values of this school and school system.

It is tempting to dismiss racist comments from students and attribute it to their age. I disagree. I think that racist comments from students demonstrate a lack of learning and understanding on the topic. To properly grasp the complexities of race, we white adults must engage in determined effort, reflection, and evaluation of our own identity development. As educators, we need to use events such as this to help students learn how to recognize and confront racism.

What can we do to stand up against racism?

Please share your thoughts with me.

While one might argue about the efficacy of this strategy, it was clear that the principal had reached that juncture at which he had to choose between courage and caution. By alerting the staff and framing the problem the way he did, the principal no doubt will receive criticism, push back, and angry commentary. Some of the critical feedback will be deserved and food for thought. Leaving this situation to be handled by the regular procedures of the school, however, would have missed an important opportunity for learning. His willingness to take the path of talking openly about a very difficult issue points to the courage of a leader.

Taking the courageous path does not mean throwing caution to the wind. In the vignette above, the principal was driven by his belief in the importance of respect within a school community. It reflected his commitment to making a decision based on a core value.

AUTONOMY VS. DEPENDENCY

So much of our work in schools is dependent on a complex network of people, resources, and contractual obligations. Any one of those domains can be a substantive roadblock to progress or, conversely, play a significant contributory role in achieving important goals. The effective leader needs to adopt a framework that abandons blame, including blame associated with insufficient resources, recalcitrant unions, and unsupportive administrators.

Leaders who aim for greatness and are willing to choose courage over caution must also adopt the belief that the desired outcome is more in their control than they may initially realize. While obstacles can no doubt block progress, effective leaders proceed with a sense of "I can do it-ness" that suggests that regardless of obstacles, the goal is achievable. It is this relentless pursuit that influences leaders to develop creative "work arounds" and alternative pathways.

In many ways, leaders must possess Dweck's growth mindset. The leader who does not grasp the full extent of her autonomy, or capacity to influence the culture, will, in the face of setbacks and defeats, lose hope and energy. Her tendency will be to blame the outcome on the faults of others. The leader who sees that her influence, while somewhat dependent on the roles that others play, is also independent of these forces will engineer solutions to problems that are encountered. The behavior of the leader with a growth mindset is not substantially different from that of the student with a growth mindset who seeks out a range of strategies to solve a difficult problem. A superintendent who finds him or herself at an impasse with the local union is dependent on the other side to reach an accord.   However, at the point of the impasse, how the superintendent responds to the difficulty is within his or her purview. We often possess more choices within a difficult situation than are easily visible. Leaders who understand that their ability to lead is linked to the interplay between autonomy and dependency often are able to find solutions where none appear to readily exist.

I did not always understand how much I could shape how I wanted to view myself. As I grew up, I received feedback from adults that led me to think of myself as being located somewhere on the "good…bad" and "smart…dumb" continuum. Like my peers, the indicators came from the kind of college one got into, the type of job one landed, and the position one established in a community. These indicators verified the extent to which one possessed the right amount of this important "stuff." In the later stages of my adulthood, I began to understand that virtue and intelligence are not static states. They are attributes that emerge from choices we make and behaviors we exhibit. On any day, we can be profoundly smart and deeply compassionate. There are also days when we our capacity for empathy appears vacant and we make poor judgments. This framework helps me understand how an "intelligent" president like Bill Clinton could make a series of unwise decisions or how "good" kids could be involved in a serious discretion. While many of us build patterns over time that are somewhat consistent, there are no guarantees about how we will choose to behave in the next moment, situation, or crisis.

While there is discomfort and pressure associated with this model of human behavior, it is liberating to know that we have the capability of breaking away from the limitations we impose on ourselves and those that we let others impose on us. In accepting this responsibility and opportunity for personal development. we can also extend it to others, most specifically children, regardless of their test scores, special education status, or socioeconomic level.

The wizardry of modern technology provides us with an ongoing reminder that human qualities are not fixed and unchangeable. No matter how technologically literate we are or are not, we have had to adapt to the concepts behind the computer age – as well as the mechanics. In many aspects of daily life, we "think" like the computer "thinks," whether putting in grades, scheduling students, charging our groceries, or banking. There are so many important capacities and tools with which we need to equip our children so that they are ready to meet the challenges that lie ahead of them. The most fundamental and timely asset we can provide is a foundational belief that their potential is rooted more in their choices, efforts, and decisions than in their prior accomplishments or defeats, their past self-image, or their lineage. Just as we once had to change our cosmic view and accept that the Earth was not at the center of our universe, we may soon come to accept that our intelligence, talents, and virtues are not fixed. We are adaptable, changeable, and capable of altering where we stand and for what we stand.

The interplay of the three sets of choices, greatness vs. maintenance, courage vs. caution, and autonomy vs. dependency, is nuanced and subtle. There are days in the lives of effective leaders when maintenance, caution, and the limiting realities of a situation dictate the pathways. There are other times, however, when one has to seize the moment and select choices that appear beyond one's grasp and without initial support. The courage that is required to make some choices can be significant.

Lesson TEN

"Leadership is an improvisational art. You may be guided by an overarching vision, clear values, and a strategic plan, but what you actually do from moment to moment cannot be scripted." Ronald Heifetz & Martin Linsky

There is no formula for success as a leader. And while utilizing Lessons One through Nine will undoubtedly raise the probability that a leader can optimize the resources within the school community, it will not guarantee improved achievement for students. Effective leadership requires incredible adaptability, improvisation, and insight. The context of each of our schools, while similar in many ways, is also quite unique. The people, the history, the latitude within contracts, the resources, the influence of local government, and the values of the district combine in distinctly unique ways to make school communities different from one another. The leader has to read the environment and adapt the lessons of leadership to the context. The task is similar to the way a jazz musician interprets music as it unfolds. In jazz, each time a song is played it is different. A skillful jazz musician uses his command of his instrument and his skillful listening to develop a unique improvisation that reflects the theme and context of the piece.

Leadership is an improvisational art

CREATIVE INSIGHTS

One of the greatest assets for a leader is creative insight. Sternberg defines insight as a "high quality solution to an ill-structured problem to which the solution is not obvious." He describes three kinds of insight that lead to creative problem solving.

1. Spotting the Pearl

Sternberg's first type of insight involves being able, in the midst of a stream of irrelevant information, to spot a pearl that can help to enhance thinking. Leaders who are astute observers of their work culture are constantly looking for creative ways to gain insight into knotty problems. I remember struggling with how best to present differentiated instruction to my staff. I wanted to address both the importance of maintaining high standards while developing reasonable and challenging alternatives to the one size fits all model that was prevalent in my building. Reading books about the topic and attending workshops helped provide me with critical knowledge. However, while attending a school band concert one evening, I realized that the band director was demonstrating, and had been doing so for years, quality differentiated instruction. All students were playing the same piece of music but in the woodwind section there were differentiated parts for the first, second, and third clarinets. The other instruments also had different scores from which they were playing. This insight allowed me to provide a common sense, familiar exemplar that gave the staff a framework on which to build a common understanding.

Another "pearl" was uncovered when I made a connection between how effective math teachers help their students solve word problems and how skillful parents help their children solve life's ill-structured problems. After becoming familiar with the research on how children think about mathematics that was done by Kate Merseth, a math educator from Harvard, I realized that I had come across a gem. Merseth asked fourth graders to respond to a problem:

There are 125 sheep and 5 dogs in a flock. How old is the shepherd?

Approximately 75% of the students produce a numerical answer to this problem. Here is one child's thinking aloud in trying to find a solution:

$125+5=130$.....this is too big, and

$125-5=120$......is still too big...while

$125 \div 5=25$. That works!

I think the shepherd is 25 years old.

This response is typical because it demonstrates the lack of sense that children have come to accept as part of their math lessons.

I remember how, as a student, I enjoyed the ease at which I would go through a worksheet of problems that varied only slightly from the example shown at the top of the page. I also remember the panic I experienced when I encountered a word problem, especially in the chapter review, that gave no clue as to the process I should use to solve it. As a new math teacher, I did not want my students to share my own lackluster history with word problems. I developed handouts for how to decipher the language of these math hurdles. "Of, in certain instances, is a signal to multiply," I explained. "If you see the word Total, it probably means you will need to add." Unfortunately, these guidelines did not adequately help my students to understand the sometimes abstract inferences within word problems. While these "hints" provided some assistance, the rules and lists did not strengthen their mathematical comprehension.

How do we get children to maintain their natural confidence in seeking patterns and using the power of their own thinking to find solutions? Too frequently, children see math as a series of strange rules and regulations that have no relationship to their own way of thinking. This perception encourages students to distance themselves from their own good judgment and to distrust their capacities. Interestingly, Jo Boaler's research indicates that the biggest difference between high achieving and low achieving math students is not innate ability or even knowledge, but rather how they think about problems. Low achievers are more rule-bound and less flexible in their thinking. High achievers rely more on their understanding and less on their memory of procedures.

If we are to make progress in math education, students must learn to trust in their own thoughtfulness and resourcefulness. It was this insight that helped me work with parents in the school community who wanted our math program to look more like the one they had as a student. Some parents believed that the new approaches we were using to instruct students lacked sufficient drill and practice. Quoting research and sharing expert views provided parents with important information, but rarely convinced them. It was through thinking about the challenge with word problems that I realized that good math teaching is not too different from skillful parenting. The ill-structured problems life presents are not too distant from those word problems. We cannot equip our kids with enough rules and guidelines to solve the variety of challenges that life presents. Our children ultimately need to be confident in their own thinking. Nurturing children's insights, intuition, and confidence to break a problem down into understandable parts is the ultimate work of both parenting and teaching.

Using Kate Merseth's "age of the shepherd" problem, we discussed with our parents the ways that children think about a problem. We all could agree that the method used by the student to solve the word problem flowed from what the student had been learning about numerical operations. Faced with a problem for which there was not enough information, the student combined insight with knowledge to arrive at the answer. With this understanding, the answer obtained by the student was reasonable. Throughout their lives, children will need to trust and rely on their thinking as well as on memorized rules.

By making this link for parents, we were able to help them appreciate our approach to mathematical instruction. They could see the connection between the approaches we used in our classrooms and their own challenges in providing their children with the confidence to be good problem solvers in life. This intellectual process will not always work when a leader is confronted with deeply skeptical parents. However, it does provide an illustration of how a leader might find creative pearls that can be hidden within our common experiences.

2. Combining Disparate Pieces of Information

The second form of insight that Sternberg describes involves seeing "how to combine disparate pieces of information whose connection is non-obvious and usually elusive." As a cultural observer, a principal must look for potential connections between and among all the arenas of school life. Allowing students to use calculators, for example, brings up concerns that they will not know the multiplication tables. Cooperative learning raises worries that students will become too dependent on their peers. Peer editing provides important feedback to the write but it enables students to "borrow" from each others' writing process.

This tension between independence and interdependence plays a strong role in education. Educators often struggle with striving for a balance between ensuring ample opportunities for students to exercise independent thought and insight while providing sufficient support to learners. They want to strike a balance between developing self-sufficiency while highlighting the benefits and importance of collaboration. Working on getting this balance just right evoked a series of memories about my school days that, in turn, led to an insight that helped me understand this challenge in a different light.

As a student, I sat in rows and worked independently. Calculators, spell checkers, and other electronic aids were not available. Rarely did I work in groups. Also rare was the opportunity to have other students enhance my thinking with their feedback. Because I have always valued being self-sufficient, in my adult life I began, reluctantly, to appreciate how the perspective of others enhanced my own. I constantly marvel at how much I benefit from having others read my writing. As a member of many committees, I am repeatedly surprised at a pattern that often recurs. I initially view a fellow committee member's radically different viewpoint with criticism and disdain. With deeper understanding, I come to appreciate how incorporating this viewpoint can improve our final product. It is amazing how often I see this scenario repeated.

As an educator, I value the independent learner who is capable of performing without assistance and in a self-directed manner. Yet, the group-oriented strategies and techniques we currently employ in schools can appear contrary to building self-sufficiency. Students often find themselves caught between the desire to be part of a group and the need to stand out as someone unique. As adults, we know that this tension doesn't go away. Our roles and responsibilities as parent, spouse, and neighbor often do not smoothly mesh with our own individual style.

Learning to coordinate our ideas and talents with those of others, seeking out the perspective of those that who think differently than we do, and becoming comfortable with both leadership and followership are part of the new set of skills that our shrinking world demands. The future is bright for those who can navigate different cultures, languages, and perspectives. Our task as leaders is to find the right balance between self-sufficiency and cooperative skills in our schools. Our children need to be prepared with the skills, information, and attitudes that will enable them to be successful in the interconnected world that they are inheriting.

3. Finding Non-Obvious Approaches to New Problems

The third kind of insight involves seeing the non-obvious relevance of old information to a new problem. As a superintendent, I needed to learn how the long-time residents of the town historically viewed the schools. This information helped in winning the confidence of the voters who, ultimately, endorsed raising additional funds for our cash strapped schools. The power of the non-obvious often emerges when one is not thinking about the problem at hand. Rather, as one is trying to solve a different problem, a connection occurs that provides a novel way of viewing a difficult situation.

This kind of connection occurred when the author Yoko Kawashima Watkins visited a school in my district. I attended her presentation to the students to show support for the people who organized this enrichment activity. Ms. Watkins shared with the students some very powerful stories about the sacrifice her parents had made to help her and her siblings survive some very challenging events. After she finished her workshop, I thanked Ms. Watkins for her presentation and we engaged in an informal conversation about modern day parenting. This conversation surprisingly helped me to link a Japanese symbol to a problem that we were experiencing within our school community.

Many parents and teachers in our school community viewed the pace of learning, teaching, and life in general as accelerating and adding stress to our lives. Parents were concerned about the stress their children were experiencing. Staff felt that no matter how fast they worked, they seemed to be falling further behind. The school year seemed more like a race that measured multitasking skills as faculty balanced school responsibilities with having enough time for sleeping, eating, and spending time with family. After I shared some of these observations with Ms. Watkins, she pulled me to a table where she grabbed a pen and a piece of paper. She drew a Japanese character on the paper that she explained was the Japanese symbol for the word "busy." It was created from two pictographs: one for the word "heart" and one for the word "kill." "Busy," she said, literally means, "to kill the heart."

LESSON TEN

Ms. Watkin illuminated for me the "nonobvious" connection between the heart and the mind. I shared this encounter with my staff and the parents in my community through a story in my newsletter that concluded:

> *As we strive to provide the best education for our students, I hope that we don't lose sight of how much success and achievement are anchored by an appreciation for and enjoyment of our children. That connection is lost sometimes from the busyness that leaves little room for the heart to inspire the mind.*

The creativity needed by a leader may emerge from a new idea or it may be a subtle adaptation of a more typical approach. It is a riff that spins the idea a little differently, related to the contours and landscape of the particular context and setting. When I first became a principal in Wellesley, MA, the school had recently reconfigured from a grade 7-9 junior high to a 6-8 middle school. The newly arrived sixth grade teachers, who came directly from the town's small elementary schools, struggled to get used to the larger building, the bell schedule, and the departmentalized approach of the school. The sixth grade teachers believed that the middle school structure did not support their students' learning. They felt that departmentalization, while having certain pedagogical advantages, weakened their relationships with students because their teaching load grew from 22 students to 95. They were frustrated because they found it difficult to get to know that many students in a deeply personal way.

There are a multitude of prescriptions for how a "genuine" middle school should be structured. As principal, I read many books and attended numerous workshops that presented "the" template for a middle school. After hours of dialogue, the teachers and I agreed that the template would not work in our context. We adopted a hybrid model that allowed the staff to teach their own homeroom nearly 60% of the time and to departmentalize for the rest of their instruction. Additionally, every sixth day, the students would have a "stay home" day, which looked like a typical day at an elementary school and in which teachers could work with students on extended learning projects. While none of these ideas represented a startlingly new approach to education, it was a challenge to develop our own adaptation of the conventional template. As the leader, my role was to listen very carefully to the teachers' dialogue and to provide "improvisational" leadership as it was needed.

Leadership also requires decision-making and moving a school toward continuous improvement. Leaders must blend analytical approaches to school improvement with practicality and creativity. It is particularly challenging to keep creativity in mind as we work under the pressures of standardized testing and federal mandates. While for many people creativity does not come easily, it is similar to other skills in that it can be practiced and strengthened.

Robert Sternberg, Dean of the Arts and Sciences College at Tufts University, has written extensively about creativity. He tells a wonderful story that illuminates a different kind of thinking in his article, "What is Successful Intelligence?"

> *Jack, who considers himself smartest in his class, likes to make fun of Irvin, the boy he has identified as stupidest in the class. Jack pulls aside his friend Tom and says, "You want to see what 'stupid' means, Tom? Watch this ... Hey, Irvin. Here are two coins. Take whichever one you want. It's yours."*
>
> *Irvin looks at the two coins, a nickel and a dime, for a while and then selects the nickel.*
>
> *"Go ahead, Irv, take it, it's yours." Jack laughs.*
>
> *Irvin takes the larger coin and walks away. An adult who has been watching the transaction from a distance walks up to Irvin and gently points out that the dime is worth more than the nickel, even though it is smaller, and that Irvin has just cost himself 5 cents.*
>
> *"Oh, I know that," replies Irvin, "but if I picked the dime, Jack would never ask me to choose between the two coins again. This way, he'll keep asking me again and again. I've already collected over a dollar from him, and all I have to do is keep choosing the nickel."*

This story reminds me that watching someone do something doesn't tell us what that person is thinking. One cannot assume that the only "good thinkers" are those who achieve academic excellence. Sometimes, some of our strongest students find it difficult to think "outside the box." At other times, those who struggle in school can be quite novel in their approach to problem solving. I worry that in the latest testing movement we have not sufficiently emphasized the importance of creative thinking. I fear that too many students are providing responses that are what they think adults want to hear, rather than providing an unusual and fresh perspective on a topic.

There have been several studies that have investigated the habits of mind that help students and adults to think creatively. Some of these *habits* are:

Tolerance for ambiguity

Students and educators sometimes dread situations in which they don't know exactly what to do. The uncertain path produces anxiety and leads some people to shut down mentally. If individuals can move beyond uncertainty as they problem solve, they will often find that an idea, solution, or approach emerges. Learning to view the anxiety as a natural part of creative problem solving is a critical habit of mind for individuals who hope to become adept at finding novel approaches to problems.

Willingness to surmount obstacles and persevere

Some students and adults fear being wrong, making a mistake, or not succeeding on the first try. Perpetual failure would wear down most people. However, individuals who can build a tolerance for temporary failure and setbacks often come to realize that their "defeats" can be their greatest ally because they indicate the aspects of thinking that need adjustment.

In our quest to bring education into the 21st Century, the pathway that helps students, teachers, and administrators understand and value different ways of thinking will be powerful. Our future leaders will need to sharpen their creative thinking and learn how to shape a culture that values many different approaches to learning and problem solving. Our collective future is not only dependent upon insuring that all our children develop math and language competencies. It will also require that they develop and apply creative ideas. In order to accomplish this lofty goal, students must work with teachers – and teachers must work with administrators – who value and model creative thinking.

Conclusion

There are many contemporary theories and frameworks that suggest how to improve education. Many of these plans call for more testing, linking teacher pay to performance, alternative pathways to teacher certification, and more business-like models for operating schools.

While any of these perspectives might lead to some improvements, I do not believe that any kind of substantive transformation will come from these interventions without paying attention to two very significant factors:

1. The training and development of skillful and dedicated teachers who can effectively meet the complex challenges of assisting a wide range of students to learn important skills and concepts.

2. The development of skillful school leaders who can support, nurture, and maintain thriving school cultures in which teachers will be excited to grow, challenge themselves, and continually work to meet the changing needs of their students.

These Ten Lessons are aimed primarily at school leadership. Leaders who pay attention to the lessons will be able to create a climate that supports the growth and improves the durability of the teaching staff. Financial remuneration continues to be an important factor in strengthening the profession of teaching, but money alone is not what teachers seek. Many educators are looking for work place cultures that are amenable to growth and development. They want their professionalism respected and their opinions and input valued. They want to be able to collaborate with colleagues on the complex issues they face.

The root word of administration is minister. Leaders who pay attention to the Ten Lessons will understand that the central responsibility of leadership is to be ministers to those who teach our students. Paul Graseck makes this point in "Where's the Ministry in Administration? Attending to the Souls of Our Schools" when he writes:

> *Teaching is humbling, hard work, often performed in isolation. It requires the wearing of many hats: manager, thinker, counselor, innovator, planner, critic, learner, diplomat, inspirer. It is a job that calls for the dexterity of a top-level executive yet is performed without the help of a secretary. Consequently, teachers yearn for support.*

Graseck goes on to explain that it is vital for leaders to "listen, comfort, support, and inspire." These "potent seeds," he suggests, "grow in the lives of teachers and students, arousing in them awe and inquisitiveness, the ground of all truth seeking and learning." The Ten Lessons align well with the ministerial support that Graseck believes that teachers need and yearn for in their daily work. Leadership requires humility and empathy as well as the strategic application of a wide range of skills and knowledge. When done effectively, leadership can make an enormous, positive difference in the professional lives of teachers and in the teaching and learning that supports adults and children in schools.

The Ten Lessons do not prescribe a formula that guarantees school improvement. Embedding them in the day-to-day routines of school life will, however, raise the probability that a system will aim itself toward continual improvement and constant renewal. A culture that nurtures a growth mind set will create the conditions for thoughtful experimentation, honest appraisals, collaborative problem solving, and creative approaches to the dilemmas and challenges that abound in schools.

ADDENDUM

The Ten Lessons form the core of a curriculum, *The DNA of School Leadership,* which is a component of the Leadership Licensure Program (LLP). The curriculum has been developed by the author in coordination with *Teachers*[21]. The LLP is a partnership of *Teachers*[21], the Massachusetts Secondary School Administrators' Association (MSSAA), and the Massachusetts Association for Supervision and Curriculum Development (MASCD). Information on *Teachers*[21] and the LLP is available at www.teachers21.org.

APPENDIX

Many of the lessons in this book emerged from my over two decades of experience as a principal. When I became a superintendent, I found that these same lessons provided an important set of guideposts on my journey from the schoolhouse to central office. The story of that transition follows to provide an additional context through which to understand the Ten Lessons of leadership.

After thirty-seven years of working as a teacher, guidance counselor, and principal, I accepted a position as Superintendent of Schools in Canton, Massachusetts on August 1, 2007. Moving from the schoolhouse to central office was both exciting and frightening. In this new role, I was a novice and a veteran simultaneously. My work as a middle school principal for twenty-two years, nineteen of which were in one community, in combination with my knowledge derived from crafting and teaching a curriculum on the DNA of Leadership, prepared me well for understanding many of the fundamental educational issues I would face as a superintendent. On the other hand, I had never worked at a central office position and I faced a multitude of challenges for which I had no prior experience.

Canton is a district of approximately 3,100 students housed in a preschool, three elementary schools, one middle school, and one high school. Approximately 10% of the families qualify for free and reduced lunch and a quickly changing student population is approximately 20% non-white. Canton, like many towns in Massachusetts, works under a legal mandate, Proposition 2½, which limits annual tax rate increases to a maximum of 2.5%. Consequently, in recent years Canton's Town Government could rarely find sufficient funds to match the rise in costs from contractual obligations, special education, utilities, and health benefits. The increases in these budget areas often averaged between 4–10% annually. This yearly "gap" between revenues and costs frequently resulted in staff reductions and the elimination of programs.

When I arrived in Canton in August, the school department was reeling from five years of "belt-tightening." In addition, the citizens had just defeated an override of Proposition 2½ that would have allowed the Town to increase its tax rate beyond 2½% and create more revenue for the schools and for municipal services. As a result of this electoral setback, the school department had to reduce twenty-two positions. In the fall of 2007, class sizes approached thirty students in a high percentage of elementary schools. The funding deficit also burdened families with a $400 fee for bus transportation and nearly $300 per sport to participate in high school athletics. There were fees for student drivers to park their cars ($150), for elementary students to participate in an after school play ($50), and for middle school students to enjoy after school activities ($100).

The middle school budget provided several examples of the strained educational scenario Canton faced. From years of staff reductions, there were so few enrichment courses that the one remaining art teacher had a student load of over 600 students. In order to fill the "holes" left in the schedule from these reductions, study halls multiplied with the largest containing 120 students who met during lunch block. This "study" was housed in the gymnasium and required young adolescents to sit on the gym floor for the period. Two middle school French classes each had thirty-eight students. The impact of the budget crisis on educational programming resulted in a less than ideal way to challenge and inspire young adolescent minds.

The funding gap also impacted contract negotiations. Five different union contracts had expired on August 31, 2007. In order to prevent further staff reductions, the School Board was not offering the teachers, custodians, secretaries, educational assistants, or food service workers a cost of living increase. Morale was low, particularly with the custodians who manned a picket line because the School Committee was seriously considering outsourcing custodial services as a means of achieving some additional savings.

The specter of a very challenging year for staff motivated a number of veteran administrators and teachers to retire, perhaps a bit earlier than they had intended. Prior to my official start, I participated in the hiring process for three principals, the Director of Curriculum, Instruction, and Technology, and five department chairs. For a relatively small district, these changes combined with a new superintendent represented significant upheaval.

In this environment I began my maiden voyage as superintendent.

I. Entry

One of the most helpful activities one can engage in when making a transition to a different job, particularly when this change involves a new district, is to develop an entry plan. One component of the plan usually involves interviewing

APPENDIX

representative individuals from the major stakeholder groups within the community. In implementing my plan, I interviewed teachers, administrators, parents, students, School Committee members and other Town officials, and citizens. I participated in nearly one hundred interviews spanning the month prior to my start in August through mid-October. Part of my entry plan involved asking three questions:

- What are the key issues facing our school system?
- What should be preserved in the town and/or the schools?
- How could I be most helpful in my role as superintendent?

While individual interviews would often branch off onto topics beyond these starting points, I raised these questions with everyone whom I interviewed. There were a number of patterns that emerged over time from these conversations. Parents were concerned about high-class sizes and expensive fees that they had to pay in order to have their children ride a bus to school or participate in athletics, intramurals, and the arts. They also expressed their perception that "bright" students and students with special needs were served better than students "in the middle." In addition to these prominent concerns, parents expressed a sense of distance from the schools. They shared their desire to be more involved with the schools but were not certain that their presence was welcome or that there was a role for them beyond fundraising. In time, this understanding of how parents felt contributed to organizing parents to develop a new political initiative that would attempt to increase the tax rate so that the schools could benefit from additional revenues.

My interviews with teachers and administrators detected a sense of sadness and disappointment that the citizenry did not appreciate nor understand the challenges they faced as educators. There was significant frustration that emerged from the lost override vote, the loss of fellow teachers whose jobs were eliminated, and the fact that the town was not willing to offer teachers a cost of living increase. Educators also expressed their frustration with the dilemma of being asked to work with much higher numbers of students while still trying to retain the standards of quality that they had delivered with lower class sizes.

The citizens had lost confidence in the leadership, judgment, and communication approaches of school officials. Some members of the town's Financial Advisory Committee felt that the school system was not sufficiently transparent with its data and information. The combination of lack of confidence and the belief that the schools were holding back information led some town officials to believe that schools' financial problems were more from mismanagement than insufficient funding.

My examination of the town's records and of newspaper accounts of previous years' exchanges between pro and anti override groups made it clear that there was a lack of dialogue and a surfeit of acrimony. In lieu of an exchange about the complexities and competing values involved in funding a good school system, there were vitriolic commentary, angry charges, and starkly drawn arguments. I took this "evidence" to be a serious symptom of an unhelpful way of communicating. In fact, as my investigations and interviews generated more data, it became clear that various constituencies were talking at each other rather than listening to one another. This communication gap was most apparent in the rift that existed between the custodial and maintenance union and the school department. The misunderstanding and mistrust between these two sides had led the school department to seriously consider outsourcing their services. As a result, the union had formed a picket line and asked for an arbiter to enter negotiations.

My sense of the frustration in the community was captured by Deborah Tannen when she wrote, "It's our tendency to approach every problem as if it were a fight between two sides. We see it in headlines that are always using metaphors for war. It's a general atmosphere of animosity and contention that has taken over our public discourse."

This data gathering exercise enabled me to learn a great deal about the town, its citizens, its needs, and most importantly, its schools. It became apparent to me that, as September drew to a close, I needed to find a way to present what I had learned to the greater community. My challenge would be to communicate this information in a manner that would not offend people or influence them to take sides. My goal would be to have stakeholders in the schools examine the data, discuss it, and reflect upon it. In a very real sense, I needed to manage a series of "difficult conversations."

I did not think it was appropriate this early in my tenure for me to initiate a campaign to raise more funds for the schools. I did begin to realize, however, that it was my responsibility to educate the community and then allow the citizens to draw their own conclusions about how best to fund the schools. While this conclusion may appear obvious, it was startling to me to conclude that I needed to use my teaching skills to complicate the thinking of the citizens. This insight provided a pivotal decision point for me - and I embraced it. I was excited about the potential of my new position but I deeply feared that the administrivia and bureaucracy of the superintendancy would trap me.

Teaching, as any skillful classroom instructor knows, is different from disseminating information. The information and data that had been presented in the past to parents, town officials, and citizens about the quality of the schools were not answering the questions of citizens or quelling their doubts about the schools and their administration. These citizens needed more than an excel spreadsheet. They needed a way to understand the "facts" and the "story" of the schools so that important ideas were well understood. Equally important, they needed to participate in communication about the schools that encouraged a civil dialogue rather than a war of words.

II. Developing Personal Relationships

One of the most important tasks that leaders must focus on as they enter a new position is the development of relationships or, as Tony Alvarado said in his early days of leadership in New York's District 2, "Relationships, relationships, relationships—it's all about relationships." I knew that when I left my principalship after nineteen years, I left behind the currency and energy that had accumulated through a wealth of relationships. My new role was not going to allow me the luxury of slowly building relationships. This aspect of my transition carried with it a sense of urgency as I began to reach out to those who had opinions and perspectives different from mine.

I channeled my recognition of the importance of building these important relationships into my writing. I crafted essays that revealed my thinking, my worries, and my struggles. These essays were published in a bi-monthly superintendent's bulletin that was electronically sent to families in the district. The following essay appeared in a December bulletin.

GAINS AND LOSSES

Whenever December rolls around I find myself looking forward to celebrating traditions with family and friends. But this month, also has a connection to a deep loss. It occurred about a dozen years ago when I was getting ready to spend vacation week at home with my family. I organized all the school papers I needed to look at during the break. I finished returning my last phone call to a parent. I sent a reply to my last unanswered e-mail. I left a list of reports for my secretary to look over while the school was empty of students and teachers. I had a sense of satisfaction over having tied up so many loose ends. I was looking forward to a little time off, a chance to spend time with my family, and an opportunity to visit my parents in New York. And then the phone rang. It was my mother's voice and she shared the sad news that my father, who had been ill, had just passed away. The joy of sharing Christmas dinner with him evaporated. Because of all of the meetings I'd managed to attend in the past month, all the tasks that I had completed, all the chores I had squeezed in, I had not been able to be there with him. So as the anniversary of the day I received that phone call rolls around, I think about time, my father, and what we want for our children.

My father died on December 22, 1995. He was 84 years old. He arrived in this country when he was ten. His name was Pellegrino D'Auria. When he started going to school he often had to clarify that Pellegrino was his first name, not his last. He got tired of explaining this, so he decided to change his name to something more American. Daniel became his new name. After completing 8th grade, my father set out to work. Although he worked hard his whole life, he never had enough money to rest easily. As a house painter, his job was seasonal. He also was scarred by the Depression because like many other people, he had lost his job. To make matters worse, news of his job loss came on the day he married my mother. These experiences led him always to worry about whether he could provide enough for his family. Keeping food on his children's plates and heat in our home were things my father worried about constantly, even when his economic condition improved.

Despite economic struggles, my father was home every single night. When it came to family dinners, his presence was as constant as the Northern star. Once my father arrived home, he rarely left. Leaving for an evening meeting was not a consideration. I have had the luxury of never being out of work and of never worrying about meeting my family's basic needs. Yet, my presence is much more erratic. Even when I am physically present at home, sometimes my mind is elsewhere. The challenge for me and my family is preserving time so that we can enjoy each other's company and have conversations that go beyond the basic, "Where are you going?" or "When do you need to be picked up?"

Ellen Goodman, a frequent contributor to the Boston Globe's editorial section, wrote an article about a family that was so busy that when the garage door accidentally landed on their cat's neck, no one had time to grieve. Important meetings and critical deadlines prevented anyone from altering their schedules. Although I may have expressed a bit of disbelief at Goodman's story, my family's experiences are a little too close to this reality for me to rest comfortably untouched by the author's remarks.

As we head deeper into a busy season and as the tasks, responsibilities and chores fill our calendars, there is a part of me that wonders about the so-called progress I sometimes think I have achieved. With too few opportunities for conversation, enjoyment, and listening to one another, I think we sometimes risk the very thing that sustains us – time to enjoy each other's company and the sharing of our how our daily adventures affect us. As one young teenager commented recently, "I don't have time to feel. Talking about feelings seems to take too much time."

My father's life has helped me to value hard work and to develop a respect for people that goes beyond their status or position. His death has led me to evaluate more critically the gains that have come to me with advanced education and economic privilege. This season will now always lead me to wonder about the gifts I have and the gifts I too easily overlook.

The early reactions to these personal expressions were skeptical. One citizen commented, "I don't quite see why the superintendent is writing about this kind of topic." I inferred that what was expected was information that focused on budgets, goals, and test scores. While these are important areas for educational leaders to illuminate, I thought that interspersing some personal writing in data centered reports could be a catalyst to jump-starting the relationship building that I wanted to achieve. By sharing aspects of my humanity, I had hoped to capture the interest and the attention of many people in the community. Over time, I began gradually to receive feedback from readers that was both appreciative and supportive of this kind of communication.

Relationships provide additional energy for a school community to solve problems, focus on improvement, and, at times, non-defensively examine its effectiveness. With this understanding in mind, I reached out to people who had been seen as critics of the school. One such person was a citizen who wrote a weekly column in the local paper and had a significant following. Another was a member of the Financial Advisory Committee who was quite critical of school financing and the schools' approach to education. I think people were surprised at first that I was interested in talking with them. When I did sit down for a cup of coffee with townspeople and school staff, I mostly listened. Taking the time to hear their perspectives helped me to understand the feelings and rationale that grounded their view of the schools. I often came away from these conversations better understanding a problem that I needed to address or a communication approach that would help me clarify an educational issue.

3. Teaching rather than informing

As I began to grasp the complexity of issues that faced the school district, the gap between needed resources and available funding was clearly the most daunting and significant need of the school system. The cumulative erosion of the quality of services, due to insufficient funding that had occurred over a five year period, left the district with very large class sizes, outdated libraries, insufficient textbooks, inadequate professional development, and diminished course offerings. While I had no doubt that efficiencies could be found in the budget, the schools needed an increase in funding. However, the slowed national economy, high utility costs, and the defeat of a recent attempt to raise taxes in the town in order to provide more dollars to the schools lowered the odds that another fiscal override vote would pass. On the other hand, the last override election lost by only 300 votes. When I examined the election results more closely, it was clear that a number of parents in the town had not voted in the last election. It appeared that making a case to the town for additional funding for the schools, while a long shot politically, was a valuable goal.

As I delved into the school's budget, I began to see value in looking for alternative ways to communicate the significant needs of the system. After examining excel spreadsheets and the minutia of the budget book, I decided that I wanted to" teach" the budget. I would not simply convey information. I would translate the budget into lessons that would engage the audience and bring about an understanding of the important ideas.

APPENDIX

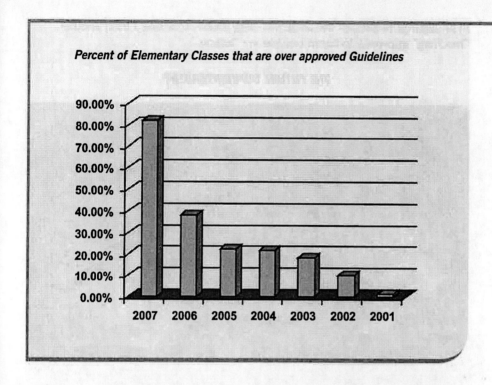

I developed a graph to illustrate some troubling trends about class size in the elementary schools. While I hoped that the graph offered a clear illustration of the hard numbers behind the data, it would not help those senior citizens who had been in classes with 40 or 50 students to understand why the trend might be concerning. The graph only told part of the story. It did little to help people understand how class size in 2008 might have a different impact on learning and teaching than it did in 1950.

TEN LESSONS IN LEADERSHIP AND LEARNING

In an attempt to deepen the understanding about class size, I tried another "teaching" approach to communicate my "lesson."

THE FUTURE SUPERINTENDENT

Can you spot the future superintendent of Canton in this 1959 photo of my fourth grade class?

There are 61 students who were part of my classroom that year. I was fortunate that this large class did little to limit my ability to succeed in school and to find meaningful employment. However, as an educator, I needed to point out that not everyone benefited from the one size fits all model that allowed class sizes to be this large. If you look "behind the scenes" of this photo, you will not be able to detect anyone with a learning disability or with special needs. If students had these needs, they would have had to attend a special school or to be educated at home. If you happen to be one of the girls in this class, your career options would be limited to the basic three: homemaker, teacher, or nurse. You also would have had little opportunity *to play organized sports. Absent from this photo are any non-white faces. If you happened to be a person of color, you more than likely would have had to attend a different school. I mention these "exceptions" because we often remember fondly the benefits of a previous era of schooling. We are less likely to view the limitations that also existed during this time. Education was not as adaptive and responsive to the range of student needs and backgrounds for which educators are currently responsible.*

One of the most powerful "learnings" from my first year was that superintendents need to convey lots of information to a variety of constituencies. Most members of these groups - parents, taxpayers, elected officials - do not have a background in education. While they all attended school, this experience does not give them the knowledge they need to understand the challenges of modern schools. School leaders need to convey to these stakeholders an array of important data. To understand the impact of special education costs on the school budget requires, for example, a mini lesson on state and Federal mandates, an explanation of autism and its dramatic increase in school populations, and a primer on the cost-benefit analysis of the value of inclusion. All of these facets of the special education budget require that the leader teach, *i.e.,* create understanding in the learner. All of what we know about good teaching needs to be brought to the lesson: the learning goal needs to be clear, the presentation needs to engage the learner, and the teacher must check for understanding, and where warranted, re-teach.

The idea of embracing teaching as a Superintendent was exhilarating. It allowed me to bridge differences and build a shared understanding of the problems and challenges in the district. While a shared understanding does not always produce effective solutions, it does increase the odds of success. It helps to remove underlying resentments and provide a common ground on which to focus community energies.

The voters of Canton decided to support an override of Proposition 2½ in May 2008 that provided an infusion of much needed resources. While there were many factors that contributed to this result that go beyond what I have described, I believe that one critical contributor was the school department's shift away from a defensive posture. In using a more open approach to communication, district leaders adopted a style that emphasized teaching rather than settling for the conveyance of information.

BIBLIOGRAPHY

Alvarado, A. (1998). "Professional Development is the Job." *American Educator.*

Barth, R. (2003). *Lessons Learned: Shaping Relationships and the Culture of the Workplace.* CA: Corwin Press.

Barth, R. (2002). "The Culture Builder." *Educational Leadership.*

Bempechat, J., London, P., & Dweck, C.S. (1991). "Children's Conceptions of Ability in Major Domains: An interview and experimental study." *Child Study Journal.*

Block, P. (1991). *The Empowered Manager: Positive Political Skills at Work.* CA: Jossey-Bass.

Boaler, J. (2009). *What's Math Got to do With It? Helping Children Learn to Love Their Least Favorite Subject.* NY: Penguin Books.

Brandt, R. (1998). *Powerful Learning.* VA: Association for Supervision & Curriculum Development.

Brandt, R. (1994). "On Creating an Environment Where All Students Learn: A Conversation with Al Mamary." *Educational Leadership.*

Byrk, A. & Schneider, B. (2002). *Trust in Schools: A Core Resource for Improvement. Russell Sage Foundation Publications.* American Sociological Association.

Chism, M. (2009). "How Effective Meetings Eliminate Workplace Drama." Retrieved from http://www.selfgrowth.com/articles/how_effective_meetings_eliminate_workplace_drama.html

D'Auria, J. & King, M. (2009). *A Principal's Dilemma.* Studies in Education. University of Chicago Publications.

D'Auria, J., King, M., & Saphier, J. (2006). *The DNA of School Leadership.* Unpublished Work.

D'Auria, John. (2001). *Factors That Influence How Children Come To Perceive their Intelligence as a Dynamic Quality.* Dissertation: U. Mass.

D'Auria, J. & Saphier, J. (1993). *How to Bring Vision to School Improvement.* Carlisle, MA: Research For Better Teaching.

D'Auria, J., King, M., & Saphier, J. *Unpublished Curriculum for Leadership Learning Program (LLP).* MA: Teachers21.

Deal, T. & Peterson, K. (2009). *The Shaping School Culture Fieldbook.* CA: Jossey Bass.

Dennison, D.R. (1996). "What is The Difference Between Organizational Culture and Organizational Climate? A native's point of view on a decade of paradigm wars." *Academy of Management Review.*

DuFour, R., Eaker, R., Karhanek, G., & DuFour, R. (2004). *Whatever It Takes: How Professional Learning Communities Respond When Kids Don't Learn.* IN: National Education Service.

Dweck, C.S. (2000). *Self-Theories: Their role in motivation, personality, and development.* PA: Psychology Press.

Elbot, C.F. & Fulton, D. (2008). *Building an Intentional School Culture: Excellence in academics and character.* CA: Corwin Press.

Evans, K.M. & King, J.A. (1992). "The Challenge of Outcome-Based Education," *Educational Leadership.*

Fullan, M. (2008). *The Six Secrets of Change.* CA: Jossey-Bass.

Fullan, M. (2002). "Principals as Leaders in a Culture of Change." Paper prepared for Educational Leadership, Special Issue, May 2002.

Ginott, Haim. (1975). *Teacher and Child: A Book for Parents and Teachers.* NY: Avon Books.

BIBLIOGRAPHY

Goleman, D., Boyatzis, R., & McKee, A. (2002). *Primal Leadership.* MA: Harvard Business School Press.

Gould, S.J. (1981). *The Mismeasure of Man.* NY: W.W. Norton and Company.

Graseck, P. (2005). "Where's the Ministry in Administration? Attending to the souls of our schools." *Phi Delta Kappan.*

Groopman, J. (2007). *How Doctors Think.* CT: Praeger Publishers.

Heifetz, R., Grashow, A., & Linsky, M. (2009). "Engage Courageously." MA: Harvard Business School Press.

Heifetz, R. (1998). *Leadership Without Easy Answers.* MA: Harvard University Press.

Henderson, V. L., & Dweck, C.S. (1990). "Motivation and Achievement." In Feldman, S. & Elliott, G.R. (Eds.), *At the Threshold:The Developing Adolescent.* MA: Harvard University Press.

Katz, L. (1982). *Reputations of Teacher Educators among Members of their Role-Set.* Paper presented at the Annual Conference of the American Educational Research Association. New York.

Lehrer, J. (2010). *How We Decide.* MA: Mariner Books.

Lucas, S. &Valentine, J. (2002). *Transformational Leadership: Principals, Leadership Teams, and School Culture.* Paper presented at the Annual Meeting of the American Educational Research Association. New Orleans.

Merseth, K. (1993)."How Old Is the Shepherd? An Essay About Mathematics Education." *Phi Delta Kappan.*

Mueller, C.M. & Dweck, C.S. (1998). "Praise for Intelligence Can Undermine Children's Motivation and Performance." *Journal of Personality and Social Psychology.*

Newmann, F.M. & Wehlage, G.G. (1995). "Successful School Restructuring: A Report to the Public and Educators." WI: Center on Organization and Restructuring of Schools.

Niemoller, M. in Mayer, M. (1995). *They Thought They Were Free: The Germans, 1933-45.* IL: Univ. of Chicago Press.

Nye, J.S. (2004). "Soft Power and Leadership." *Compass: A Journal of Leadership.*

Obama, B. (2009). Speech at Cairo University. Cairo, Egypt.

Olson, K. (2009). *Wounded by School: Recapturing the Joy in Learning and Standing Up to Old School Culture.* NY: Teachers College Press.

Reeves, D.B. (2004). *Assessing Educational Leaders.* CA: Corwin Press.

Senge, P. et. al. (1994) *The Fifth Discipline Fieldbook: Strategies and Tools for Building a Learning Organization.* NY: Random House, Inc.

Sternberg, R. (1996). "What Is 'Successful' Intelligence?" *Education Week.* http://www.edweek.org/ew/articles/1996/11/13/11stern.h16.html?print=1

Sternberg, R.J. & Lubart, T.I. (1991). "Creating Creative Minds." *Phi Delta Kappan*

Stone, D., Patton, P., Heen, S., & Fisher, R. (2000). *Difficult Conversations. How to Discuss What Matters Most.* NY: Penguin Books.

Suskind, R. (2004). *The Price of Loyalty: George W. Bush, the White House and the Education of Paul O'Neill.* NY: Simon and Schuster Paperbacks.

Tannen, D. (2001). I Only Say This Because I Love You. NY: Random House

Yerkes, R.M. (ed.) (1921). "Psychological Examining in the United States Army." *Memoirs of the National Academy of Sciences, vol. 15.*

Wheatley, M. (2002). *Turning to One Another: Simple Conversations to Restore Hope to the Future/Willing to be Disturbed.* CA: Berrett-Koehler Publishers.

About Teachers[21]

Teachers[21] is a national non-profit organization dedicated to systemic education reform. The mission of Teachers[21] is to ensure that every student learns from effective and caring teachers and that every school is guided by competent and resolute leaders. To accomplish these goals, we offer robust professional development opportunities, research promising practices, and pursue policy initiatives that establish rigorous standards, institutional structures of support, and accountability for all educators.

Teachers[21] is reshaping the profession of teaching and school leadership through four major programmatic areas:

PROFESSIONAL DEVELOPMENT

Since 1993, Teachers[21] has built a reputation as a key provider of knowledge-based professional development to educators nationally and across New England, including over 50% of the districts in Massachusetts.

RESEARCH, PROGRAM DEVELOPMENT, AND DISSEMINATION

Teachers[21] develops and disseminates new knowledge and innovative programs that advance PreK-12 teaching, leadership, and learning.

> **The Leadership Licensure Program (LLP)** is a state-approved program that is preparing its thirteenth cohort of aspiring principals. This program provides a comprehensive approach, based on the needs of the field that integrates and aligns rigorous curricula, practicum experiences, and portfolio assessments. The cumulative effect for students is a rich array of learning opportunities that will prepare them for the enormous complexities of school leadership. Teachers[21] created this program in partnership with the Massachusetts Secondary School Administrators' Association (MSSAA) and the Massachusetts Association for Supervision and Curriculum Development (MASCD).

The Leadership Licensure Program for Superintendents (LLPS) is an outgrowth of the LLP. The continued demand for district administrators and the success of the Leadership Licensure Program for school based administrators led *Teachers*[21] to partner with the Massachusetts Association of School Superintendents (MASS) and Boston College on the development of a licensure/doctoral program. Additionally, Massachusetts Secondary School Administrators Association (MSSAA) and Massachusetts Association of Supervision and Curriculum Development (MASCD) continue to be partners with us on this new and exciting initiative.

The Leadership Coaching Model promotes and sustains excellence in leadership to support instruction and learning for successful student achievement. This key reform strategy focuses on a systemic approach to meeting the goals of a district and/or school. Coaching works at the individual, school district team and district network levels to serve as a proactive catalyst for professional learning rather than reactive and remedial approach. The heart of our Leadership Coaching is collaborative reflective inquiry. A variety of mentoring, supervisory and peer relationships allow the challenges of day to day practices to be successfully addressed.

In 1999, *Teachers*[21] and Simmons College co-founded **The Beginning Teacher Center** to create a seamless continuum of professional supports for teachers from their pre-service training throughout their first three years of teaching. At the heart of the center's approach is a comprehensive induction model that *Teachers*[21] developed over ten years in working with school districts to help them systematically grow new teachers into skillful practitioners. The three goals of the BTC are: 1) encourage all school districts to understand and implement the comprehensive model of beginning teacher induction, 2) create a seamless continuum through teacher preparation and the first three years of practice, and 3) become a national force that moves the American education establishment to devote attention and resources to the induction of beginning teachers.

Our Comprehensive Induction Model surrounds the beginning teacher with support, accountability, and a force for constant improvement of teaching and learning in their classrooms. It further includes school board policy and structures to sustain the effectiveness of the program. A rigorous broad-based planning process is married to an ongoing communication plan that ensures widespread ownership. The key beliefs that serve as the basis for this model and drive the center's work are: 1) the success of the beginning teacher is the responsibility of all staff at the school, 2) well-designed induction is essentially excellent staff development, and 3) effective induction programs inherently work to transform the culture of the school.

Teachers[21] provides **School Turn Around and Redesign Support** and has been pre-qualified by the DESE as a vendor to support the 11 Essential Conditions for School Effectiveness. *Teachers*[21] provides district and school strategic planning, consultation, and process facilitation to support the ability of school districts to engage in systemic school and district improvement. These services encompass the eleven essential conditions for school effectiveness and include:

- Rigorous, research-based staff development for administrators and teachers in academic disciplines, content specific pedagogies, general pedagogical knowledge and skills, children and their differences, professional culture, parent and community involvement, instructional leadership, organizational leadership, strategic leadership and community leadership

- Executive coaching for district and school administrators

- Consultation on data-driven planning and evaluation, professional development, induction, and school and district improvement planning

- Planning facilitation including strategic planning, professional development, assessment, induction, content and instructional technology.

- Job embedded support, which includes co-teaching, classroom demonstrations, modeling for educators in their classrooms, and working with teams.
- Leading a school and district improvement process

The **Urban District Improvement Model** consists of ten change actions that create a comprehensive, transferable model for achieving district-wide improvements in professional culture, instructional practice, and student learning. This flexible model creates a unique framework that will adapt to the context-specific conditions of a district and will complement and support its change agenda. *Teachers*[21] serves as a "reform support organization" providing advisors, critical friends, honest brokers, and trainers to implement the model.

Teachers[21] implements its **Secondary School Re-Design Model** to help school districts improve the educational experiences available to their high school students and ensure they have the skills and knowledge they need to live productive, meaningful lives after graduation. This flexible model addresses a gap in many high school reform approaches, which focus primarily on re-structuring (an important precondition to improvement), by intensively addressing what teachers and administrators know and can do for students. This model places a particular focus on helping high schools to strengthen and integrate their curriculum improvement and NEASC processes with all the other elements of school reform.

Our **Middle School Re-Design Model** is a Learning Laboratory that has been co-designed with a school district to embed the beliefs and practices of integrated learning and standards based programs into the district's middle schools. With the competing interests of high stake testing and the social and emotional needs of the emerging adolescent, middle schools are struggling to maintain the concept of educating the whole child. The *Teachers*[21] model utilizes our coaching model and our professional learning community practices to coordinate the design and development of shared expectations and outcomes resulting in a rigorous challenging common core curriculum for all middle school students.

The **Masters Program in Mathematics Education** is a unique partnership between *Teachers*[21] and Simmons College. This program provides participants with the knowledge of math and pedagogical content, inquiry-based instruction, research-based strategies to use in classrooms today, and the infusion of 21st century skills.

Through our **Professional Learning Communities** initiatives, *Teachers*[21] offers a wide array of services to help districts, schools, grades or departments develop collaborative practices to monitor and encourage increased student success. According to Eastwood and Lewis, "Creating a collaborative culture is the single most important factor for successful school improvement initiatives and the first order of business for those seeking to enhance the effectiveness of their schools." The development of a professional learning community can take many paths and our services, based on the *Teachers*[21] model, include a two-day foundational institute, one day essential concept workshops, full 36-hour graduate courses or coaching for small groups, teams, or individuals.

Teachers[21] **Publications** promote emerging trends and cutting-edge thinking that advance the knowledge bases of professional practice:

> **"Beyond Mentoring: Putting an Instructional Focus on Comprehensive Induction Programs, 3rd Edition",** by Jon Saphier, Susan Freedman and Barbara Aschheim, describes the comprehensive induction model and links it intimately with an instructional focus. This model is at the heart of the Beginning Teacher Center and its work in districts.

"Assessment in Practice: A View from the School", by Lynn F. Stuart, describes a system of school-based assessment in the context of building and sustaining a professional learning community that focuses on improving student learning.

"Discovering New Horizons: Leadership Coaching for the 21st Century Principal", by Paul Akoury and Ron Walker, highlights the *Teachers*[21] Model of Leadership Coaching and provides a resource for what instructional leadership that improves teaching and learning can look like in practice.

"Voices from the Field: Conversations with Mentors and New Teachers", by Virginia Tang, provides 25 classroom-based vignettes that can be used to stimulate productive discussion about a broad range of classroom issues that face the new teacher. These vignettes portray elementary, middle, and high school scenarios, present real dilemmas that can be the jumping off point for conversations. This publication is a product of the Beginning Teacher Center of *Teachers*[21] and Simmons College.

"Mentoring Works: A Sourcebook for School Leaders", by Lynda Johnson, Susan Freedman, Barbara Aschheim and Vicki Levy Krupp, focuses on the mentor and new teacher relationship. What role should principals play? How should mentors be chosen and evaluated? What are the key components of a successful mentoring program? Mentoring Works examines these and other questions through current, readable research and literature on induction. Journal articles are complimented with practical strategies and suggestions for supporting new teachers. This publication is a product of the Beginning Teacher Center of *Teachers*[21] and Simmons College.

ABOUT *TEACHERS*[21]

PUBLIC DISCOURSE

Teachers[21] improves public understanding about the significance and complexities of knowledge-based teaching and administration in schools by informing legislators, policymakers, opinion shapers, and business community leaders.

POLICY

Teachers[21] influences policymakers to align the ten personnel processes that impact teacher and administrator quality. At the state level, we work with legislators and staff, K-16 practitioners, and the business community to generate legislative proposals that will improve educator quality for all children in Massachusetts Public Schools. At the national level, *Teachers*[21] partners with organizations such as The National Commission on Teaching and America's Future and The National Board for Professional Teaching Standards to influence discussions about policy and practice relating to educator quality.

For additional information, please visit our website at www.teachers21.org.

ABOUT THE AUTHOR

John D'Auria's educational experience has spanned four decades and many roles: math teacher, guidance counselor, principal, and superintendent. He has worked with hundreds of school leaders in urban and suburban settings on developing a vibrant school culture, managing conflict in the workplace, and sharpening the academic focus of school teams. John's educational research has focused on how the assumptions that people hold about intelligence significantly influence their learning. He is the author of a curriculum, "The DNA of School Leadership", and co-author of *How to Bring Vision to School Improvement*. John has published a number of articles including "The Superintendent as Teacher," *Phi Delta Kappan Online Edition,* Fall, 2009; "A Principal's Dilemma," jointly with Matt King, *Schools: Studies in Education,* University of Chicago Press, Spring, 2009; and "3 Strands Form Strong School Leadership," jointly with Jon Saphier and Matt King, *National Staff Development Council,* Spring, 2006.

John is the President of *Teachers*[21] and a frequent speaker at educational conferences. He welcomes your comments and insights related to this book and can be reached at jdauria@teachers21.org.